# Homemade Breads

MODERN PUBLISHING
A Division of Unisystems, Inc.
New York, New York 10022

**Abbreviations used in this book:**
c. = cup
tbsp. = tablespoon
tsp. = teaspoon
oz. = ounce
lb. = pound
in. = inch
hr. = hour
min. = minute
sec. = second

Published by Modern Publishing, A Division of Unisystems, Inc.

Text © 1985 Joshua Morris, Inc.
Illustrations: A/S Hjemmet 1979

Printed in Denmark

# Contents

rises above 100°, the rising takes place too quickly and the baked product will have large, irregular holes. At 120–130° the yeast cells die and the dough will not rise at all. Yeast may be bought fresh or dried. Fresh yeast is soft, smooth and grayish white in color. A white coating on fresh yeast does not affect its leavening properties, but stale yeast with cracks and brown edges should not be used.

There are two methods for using dry yeast. One is to dissolve it in liquid; the other is to mix it in directly with the flour. Follow the directions on the package. Fresh yeast can only be kept for a limited time and must be refrigerated. It may be frozen but must be thawed out before it is used. Dry yeast will keep for a long time, provided it is kept in a cool, dry place and the package is kept tightly closed after use.

### Sourdough

In the old days, sourdough was used all the time. A lump of yeast dough from baking day was kept in a cool place to be used for the next baking. This is a procedure which can well be used today in households where baking is done regularly. The "sourdough" is stirred into the liquid being added to the dough at the next baking, possibly with the addition of a little new, fresh yeast.

Sourdough can be made by stirring flour and water or sour milk together. It ferments naturally so that after 24–48 hr. the sourdough is ready to use.

# The Ingredients and the Oven

*Bread is an important part of our diet. It contains many of the proteins and other nutrients we need. The coarser the bread, the more beneficial it is for our teeth, our digestion and, in fact, for our whole body.*

There are many advantages in doing your own baking; it is both economical and good-tasting, and there are many more possibilities of varying the types of bread. Bread baking once or twice a week can be fitted into the working routine of almost everyone. The actual baking is enjoyable too, and so are the delicious aromas which pervade the kitchen.

It pays to make large quantities while you are at it. The work is about the same and you save energy by making full use of a hot oven.

Read about large-quantity baking on pages 60–61, and how to freeze bread on pages 62–63.

### About Baking

Bread is usually made of yeast, flour, salt, and liquid, but there is great scope for variation by using different types of flour and by the addition of different flavors.

Here is some information regarding different ingredients and their properties.

### Yeast

Yeast consists of living, microscopic cells which develop when liquid, carbohydrates, and protein are added. During this process, released carbon dioxide causes the dough to rise. The ideal temperature for the yeast cells is between 80° and 85°. If the temperature is lower, it takes longer for the dough to rise. For cold rising, only half the amount of yeast is used and all the ingredients should be kept at 50°. In the refrigerator, rising will then take approximately 8 hr. If the temperature in the dough

## Liquid

Water, buttermilk, fresh or sour milk, or beer, are customarily used for yeast baking. The temperature must not be over 100° for the sake of the yeast cells. The whole dough will then have a temperature of approximately 80–85°. Bread and cakes made with milk will not be as light as those made with water, but neither will they dry out as quickly.

## Fats

A little butter, margarine, oil, or other fat in the dough will keep all kinds of bread fresh longer. Small amounts of fat can be melted into the required liquid, but if a lot of butter is called for in the recipe, this should be crumbled into the flour or rolled into the dough after it has risen once. Follow the recipe.

## Flour

Wheat flour, of all the various types of flour, is the most suitable for baking and therefore is often mixed with other flours. When wheat flour is mixed with liquid at the right temperature, gluten is formed. Gluten is an elastic substance which binds the carbon dioxide freed by the yeast. The viscous gluten threads hold the dough together, the starch in the flour fills it out and the yeast makes it rise. The degree of moisture in flour varies and consequently so does its capacity to absorb moisture. Therefore, always hold back a little of the flour until you see how much liquid is being absorbed. The dough should just pull away from the sides of the bowl when enough moisture has been absorbed. If you use too much flour, the baked bread will be hard and dull.

## Eggs

Eggs vary a great deal in size and quality, but in recipes where the number of eggs is given, if nothing else is mentioned, Grade A large is intended. Eggs which are to be used for brushing over the top of buns or bread made with yeast may be beaten with a little milk to make them go farther.

## How to Use the Oven

Most ovens have thermostats, but they are not always entirely accurate. If there is any deviation between the temperature and baking time given in a recipe and that which is registered on your own oven, make a note on this beside each recipe. Oven heat and baking time are different for large loaves of bread, small rolls, cakes, buns, etc. The main rule is that small things are baked at higher temperatures than large things. Large loaves and cakes are placed low down in the oven, small rolls and buns, etc. are baked on the middle rack.

When loaves and cakes have risen completely they should be brushed with beaten egg or sprinkled with seeds or flour, according to the recipe. Start heating your oven when the dough has finished rising for the first time, then it will be at the right temperature when the dough has finished rising for the second time. Bread continues to rise for a while after it has been put in the oven. In order to avoid too hard a crust forming at once, a small pan filled with warm water may be placed on the bottom of the oven. The crust will be extra crisp if the bread is brushed with water a few times during the baking.

| Oven Temperatures | °F |
|---|---|
| Cool | 225 |
| Cool | 250 |
| Very slow | 275 |
| Slow | 300 |
| Moderately slow | 325 |
| Moderate | 350 |
| Moderately hot | 375 |
| Moderately hot | 400 |
| Hot | 425 |
| Very hot | 450 |
| Very hot | 475 |
| Extremely hot | 500 |

## Measuring and Weighing

Although it might seem easier and quicker to measure, weighing the ingredients gives a much more accurate result. However, standard measuring spoons can be purchased as sets. The spoonfuls should always be level to give the correct measurement.

It is not always necessary to weigh butter or margarine for baking as a small error either way will not make much difference. And, of course, butter and margarine are frequently sold in $\frac{1}{4}$ lb. sticks that measure 8 tbsp., or $\frac{1}{2}$ c.

## Keeping and Freezing

Instructions on keeping and freezing yeast bread and cakes are found on pages 62–63.

# When You Bake . . .

Bread made from fermenting dough has been known for thousands of years. But it was only two or three centuries ago that yeast, as an ingredient, came to be used to speed up the successful but time-consuming sourdough method, with its slow leavening. At one time people made yeast at home from hops or beer leavings – with very variable results. Nowadays, most bread comes from large commercial concerns, but more and more people are making it themselves. For reasons of both taste and healthy eating, they want to try out the different flours available from the coarsest rye to the lightest white.

Baking yeast bread and cakes is a craft that requires practice for good results. There are tricks to be learned, but once you get the hang of it, there is nothing to it. Even though the recipes in this book on yeast baking are as exact as possible, you can be unlucky, so read the following tips and advice on yeast baking in general. Don't be discouraged if the result the first time isn't quite what you had hoped for – perhaps the flour was a little too cold, even that can be enough to rob you of success.

## 10 Good Tips

1. Let all the ingredients you are going to use stand at room temperature in the kitchen for a couple of hours. Even a cold bowl can cool the dough sufficiently to prevent rising from taking place as it should.

2. Yeast dough mustn't stand at too low a temperature or in a draft, either when it is being kneaded or while it is rising.

3. Never introduce yeast to salt or sugar on their own. Yeast should be dissolved in tepid or room-temperature liquid. If you mix yeast directly into the flour, both the yeast and the flour should have stood for a couple of hours in the kitchen.

4. If you have an electric mixer which is powerful enough for yeast doughs, only half the flour should be added together with the other ingredients. Do not let the machine knead for more than 3–5 min. at a time. If you let it knead longer, the dough will not rise properly. The rest of the flour can be kneaded in by hand.

5. In a recipe using both coarse and fine flour, the coarse should be added first and the fine afterward. Do not add all the flour at once, for flour does not absorb moisture equally at all times. Absorption can vary according to the moisture in the flour after being stored, etc.

6. The oven should always be preheated to the desired temperature before the bread or cakes are put in, unless otherwise indicated in the recipe.

7. Baked bread, when ready to be taken out of the oven, gives a special hollow sound which is easily recognizable when you tap the bottom of the loaf with your fingers. Bread which is baked in a tin should preferably be taken out of the tin and baked on the oven rack or a baking sheet for the last 10–15 min.

8. Bread and cakes should normally be cooled on a rack. This releases the steam and the baked product stays dry. Certain breads (especially the coarse types) can be cooled under a cloth for a softer crust and consistency.

9. Preferably use a timer when you are baking and while the yeast dough is rising. Make a note on your recipes if the temperatures and times given do not correspond with your stove.

10. Do not open the oven door too early and on no account let it bang shut when you close it, as the resulting draft is enough to cause the bread or cake to collapse.

## If you should be unlucky . . .

*The dough did not rise properly*
The liquid was too warm – or too cold.

The rising dough was standing in a draft.

The yeast was too old, and had become dry or crumbled.

*The dough collapsed*
The dough was left to rise too long the second time.

*The bread has big or irregular holes*
The dough was not kneaded enough after the first rising.

*The bread is hard*
Too much flour in the dough.

The dough did not rise properly.

*The bread is heavy*
Too little flour in the dough.

The dough did not rise enough or the temperature was too warm during the rising period.

*The bread is cracked*
The dough rose too quickly.

The dough should have been pierced or cut into before baking.

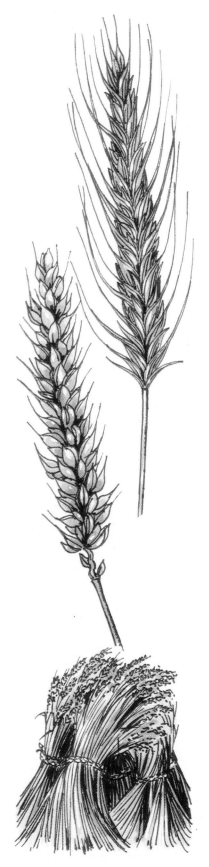

# Grain Becomes Flour

*Bread has always made up a considerable part of our daily food, and experience has shown that grain products make a good basis for general well-being, health, and working capacity. For many thousands of years, mankind has cultivated grain. Formerly, it was a condition for permanent settlement because grain made people independent of a vagrant, roaming existence with its constant search for, and collection of, food. Well-filled storehouses of grain provided security against bad years and famine.*

The principal grains are oats, wheat, and rye. Wheat is the staple grain in our diet and, in one form or another, the constituent of most breads. Rye is an important grain too for bread making but needs the gluten in wheat flour to rise. Never use rye flour alone.

The most important part of the grain plant is the grain itself. It consists of the husk (bran), the germ and the endosperm (starch). The husk makes up 15 percent of the weight of the grain and protects the germ. The latter is just inside the husk and makes up only 3 percent of the weight. The endosperm is the main part of the grain. It makes up around 82 percent of the weight. The ripe grain contains elements from all the main groups of foodstuffs: the energy-providing carbohydrates; proteins and fats; minerals; and vitamins.

## Flours Used in Yeast Baking
The names for commercially produced breads, indicating what flour was used in the baking, are numerous. Basically, home-baking bread flours, except for oatmeal, are as follows:

All-purpose white flour made from wheat
Rye flour (mixed with wheat)
Wheatmeal flour
Wholewheat flour
Wholegrain rye flour

These, on their own, or in various combinations, provide a fascinating variety of breads, cakes, and pastries with yeast as the raising agent.

## How is Flour Made?
Any number of different kinds of flour can be made, but two main groups are distinguishable, namely *refined flour* and *whole-ground flour*. Refined flour is made from the starchy part of the grain. The husk and the germ are sifted away, and the flour is very light or white in color.

Whole-ground flour is made by crushing the entire grain which contains the husk, the germ, and the kernel. Nothing is removed in the grinding process.

The term fine and coarse refers to whether the grain is finely or coarsely ground, but both contain the whole grain with the husk, the germ, and the kernel.

## Wheat Flour
Wheat flour is the type most often used. It is used alone or mixed with other flours. Its baking properties are improved when the flour is stored for a while after it is ground, as the flour needs time to mature.

White flour has a low extraction rate, something like 70 percent, meaning that little except starch is left, the husk and the germ are largely discarded. It is also often bleached. Soft cake flour, while best for some forms of baking, lacks the gluten desirable for making bread. Bread flour, which is "hard" flour milled from grain grown in cooler areas of the country, contains more gluten and should be used if possible. All-purpose flour on most grocery shelves is a blending of soft and hard flour and is fine for bread baking.

Wheatmeal flours have an extraction rate of about 85–90 percent and are flours with the bran partly removed. They produce a lighter, moister loaf than wholewheat flours.

The terms wholemeal and wholewheat are, to a large extent, synonymous, being better differentiated by the coarseness and method of the milling. Stone-ground flour, for instance, is coarse with a distinct flavor, and milled in the old way between millstones instead of roller milled. Wholemeal and wholewheat flours are of 100 percent extraction, i.e. the whole of the wheat grain is used.

## Rye Flour
Rye has weaker baking properties than wheat and for this reason wheat flour is often added to it when it's sold to improve its baking properties. The various kinds of flour are mixed with each other to create variations in baking products, but wheat flour is the essential element due to its gluten content.

## Storing Flour
As a general rule, flour should be kept in a dry, cool place well away from strong-smelling food.

Shelf life depends on the amount of water in the flour but, on the whole, flour may well be considered a non-perishable food. Under proper storage conditions wheat and rye flours can be kept up to two years without deteriorating in quality. Wholewheat flours have a much shorter life than white flours because the germ retained in the wholewheat contains fat which can become rancid. It also normally keeps a shorter time in summer than in winter. The best containers are enamel cannisters or jars with tight-fitting lids. When you buy flour, the package is always of paper. Paper allows the moisture to escape and prevents the flour from forming lumps; nevertheless, for the best result, flour should be sifted before being added, as directed in a particular recipe. Some brands of flour are much finer than others.

*Sacks of grain and flour – we have many possibilities to choose from when we start to bake. Mixing coarse and fine types provides any number of variations of bread, cakes, and rolls.*

# Working with Yeast

*Baking with yeast may be divided into the following steps – dough making, rising, kneading, the second rising and, finally, baking. This book contains recipes for all kinds of breads and cakes, but first we shall deal with the two methods used in the basic recipes for the most common types of bread.*

### Everyday Bread (basic recipe)
2 oz. active dry yeast
1 c. + 2 tbsp. water
2 tbsp. butter
2 tsp. salt
2–2½ c. rye flour
2–2½ c. all-purpose flour
suitable for freezing

Follow method 1, page 11, and bake in a standard 8 by 4½ in. loaf tin. Brush with water and prick before baking.
Bake for about 50 min. at 400°.

### Kneipp Bread (basic recipe)
1 oz. active dry yeast
1 c. + 2 tbsp. water
1–2 tsp. salt
2 tbsp. oil
1–1½ c. rye flour
1–1½ c. wholewheat flour

Follow method 1, page 11, and bake in a standard 8 by 4½ in. loaf tin. Brush with water and prick.
Bake for about 40 min. at 400°.

### Whole-grain Bread (basic recipe)
2 oz. yeast
1 c. boiling water
2 tsp. salt
1 tbsp. butter
1–1½ c. stone-ground whole-wheat flour
¼ c. rye flour
2–2½ c. all-purpose flour
¼ c. whole grains

Follow method 1, page 11, and bake in a standard 8 by 4½ in. loaf tin. Put 1 oz. grain to soak in the boiling water for about 2 hr. Add to the dough. Sprinkle 1 oz. grain on top of the loaf. Brush with water and make a few slashes on top.
Bake for about 40 min. at 400°.

### Graham Bread (basic recipe)
2 oz. yeast
1 c. milk
¼ c. butter or margarine
1 tsp. salt
1 tsp. sugar
3–3½ c. whole-wheat flour
2–3 c. all-purpose flour

Follow method 1, page 11, and bake in a 2-lb. loaf tin. Brush with water and prick before baking.
Bake for about 30 min. at 400°.

### Homemade Bread (basic recipe)
2 oz. yeast
1 tbsp. oil
1 tsp. salt
2 c. skimmed milk
2 c. stone-ground whole-wheat flour
1 c. rye flour
2–3 c. all-purpose flour

*1. For the sponge method, put crumbled fresh yeast or dried yeast in a hollow in the flour.*

*2. Dissolve the yeast in tepid liquid, and stir in a little of the flour to make a sponge.*

*3. The sponge should look like this when it has risen for about 15 min.*

*4. Add seasonings and melted, cooled butter or other fat.*

*5. Stir the dough vigorously so that it becomes shiny and smooth.*

Follow method 1, page 11, and bake in a standard 8 by 4½ in. loaf tin. Brush with sweetened coffee and cut a deep slit lengthwise.
Bake in a 2-lb. loaf tin at 400° for about 1 hr.

## Method 1 (Dissolved Yeast)

1. In this method we start by dissolving and proofing the yeast in tepid liquid. If the yeast is active, as it should be, the liquid will bubble and foam after 5–10 min. A little sugar speeds the process. Salt retards it and should never be added at this point. Once the yeast is proofed, it should be added to the flour. Then, other ingredients should be added. The method is equally good for all types of yeast baking. The illustrations opposite show the dissolved yeast being poured into the flour, but sometimes a large bowl is used at the start to dissolve the yeast in and the flour, etc. added to the yeast.

2. Melt the butter and let it cool until it is the same temperature as the other ingredients. Then add salt and eggs, sugar and other ingredients. If the butter amount is greater than 10–15 percent of the flour, the butter should be rubbed into the flour before the liquid is poured in. In some recipes, however, cold butter is rolled into the dough after the first rising.

3. Stir the dough thoroughly until it is smooth and elastic. If you are using a mixer with a dough hook, add only half the flour and do not let the machine run for more than 3–5 min. Then work the rest of the flour into the dough on a floured work sur-face. Knead it thoroughly. Use the heels of your hands to push the dough away from you. Gather it back and repeat this motion until the dough no longer clings to the board or to your hands.

4. Put the dough back into the bowl, cover it and put it in a warm place, away from any draft. Yeast dough must never stand in a draft and never be placed on any direct heat, unless this is stated specifically in the recipe. You can sprinkle a thin layer of flour over the bowl to prevent a dry film from forming. If the yeast dough is oily, a cloth can be moistened and wrung out and placed on top. Or put the bowl in a plastic bag. The dough has finished rising when it has doubled in bulk – usually 1–2 hours later. Turn it out onto the work surface, punch it down and knead it lightly.

5. If the dough is to be divided, do this now, and let the portions stand for 3–5 min. before you begin to work with them. This allows the elastic gluten threads to contract, so that the dough is easier to roll out. If, for example, you have divided the dough into three to make braided bread, hold the strips up for a moment by one end. Then the pieces of dough will not contract when they are rolled out. If no other procedure is mentioned in the recipe, the dough should be left to rise again in a tin or on a baking sheet for about 20 min. Before it is put in the oven, it should be brushed over, slit, sprinkled, etc., according to the recipe.

6. Bread and large cakes should be baked on the lowest rack in the oven; buns and rolls in the middle. If you use waxed paper on the baking sheet or in the tin, it is not necessary to grease the sheet or tin as well. The paper will not stick and it can be used several times. It also simplifies cleaning.

Bread and cakes cooked in tins can be taken out of the tin and placed directly on a baking sheet for the last 10–15 min. if the bottom and sides are too light in color. Tap the bread with your finger – if there is a hollow sound, it is baked through. Place the baked bread or cake on a wire rack. This lets the steam come out and the bread will not be damp on the bottom.

If the bread or cake is to be frozen, wrap it in foil while it is lukewarm, and put it in the freezer when it is completely cool. This way the crust will not fall off thawed. Bread and cakes can be thawed out in their wrapping at room temperature, but buns and rolls should be thawed and warmed in the oven at 400°.

## Method 2 (Sponge)

1. When baking with yeast, it is worth stressing again that all ingredients and equipment must be at room temperature. If, for example,

6. After the dough has been allowed to rise for about 15 min., it should look like this, plump and springy.

7. Twine three long "sausages" of dough into braided dough. Fold the ends in under the bread.

8. The bread rises for the second time, is brushed (with egg, etc.) and put in the preheated oven until done.

the flour is too cold, the dough will rise slowly and poorly. Therefore, let everything sit out for a couple of hours before baking. Always sift the flour; not only will it be lighter but the temperature will be even.

The amount of flour in any particular recipe can never be given entirely accurately, as the amount of moisture in flour varies; but it is a good rule not to use all the flour to begin with and then add more if necessary. This way, you should be able to avoid too dry a dough. Make a hollow in the flour and put in the crumbled fresh or dried yeast.

2. Warm milk or water until it is lukewarm (about 95°). If it is more than a few degrees warmer than 113°, the yeast cells will be killed and the dough will not rise. It is better to dissolve the yeast in too cold liquid than too warm. Pour the liquid slowly over the yeast and stir in a little of the flour. Sprinkle a thin layer of flour

over the top, cover the bowl with a cloth or large plastic bag and let it stand in a warm, draft-free place for about 15 min.

3. When the sponge has finished rising, there will be cracks in the flour which was sprinkled on top. Proceed as in Method 1, steps 2–6.

### White Bread (basic recipe)

(makes 1 large loaf or 24 rolls)
Preparation time: 15 min.
Rising time: about 15 min.
Baking time and oven temperature: bread, 35 min. at 400°; dinner rolls, 12–18 min. at 425–475°.
Put large loaf on the lowest rack and dinner rolls on the middle rack in the oven.
Suitable for freezing

$\frac{1}{2}$ oz. yeast
2 tsp. salt
1 tbsp. butter or margarine
1 c. water or milk
2–3 c. all-purpose flour

1. Heat the water or milk to 95–100°. Dissolve the yeast in the liquid. Add to most of the flour. Stir and add melted butter and salt. Work the dough thoroughly with a wooden spoon or in an electric mixer, and knead in the rest of the flour with your hands. Cover the dough, put it in a warm place and let it rise for about 40–60 min.

2. Turn the dough out and knead well on a floured board. Shape into a large loaf or 24 dinner rolls and let them rise again under a cover for 10–20 min.

3. Brush over with cream, milk or beaten egg and slit the loaf with a sharp knife. Dinner rolls may also be slit, but this is only for decoration (see illustrations, page 16).

4. Allow about 35 min. baking time at 400° for a large loaf made with this basic dough; for rolls, 12–18 min. at 425–475°. The oven should be heated in advance before the rolls are put in. A large loaf should be baked on the lowest rack, rolls on the middle

rack of the oven. This basic dough can be used for unsweetened buns, crescents, etc., as well as for white bread and rolls.

### Time-table for Freshness

For all recipes the time you need for baking is given. If you want to serve baked products as fresh as possible, count back from the time you want to serve them, subtract time for cooling, baking, rising and preparation, and you will arrive at the exact time you should start. This applies particularly to baked items such as braids, buns, crescents, etc., which can be served warm.

### Yeast Dough Step by Step

*1. Sprinkle dried yeast or fresh, crumbled yeast into lukewarm liquid (95– 100°F) and stir. It is simplest to dissolve the yeast in a little of the liquid, then add the remaining liquid afterward. A white film on fresh yeast does not affect its rising properties, but if the yeast is dried out, cracked and had brown edges, it should be thrown away.*

*2. Mix together most of the flour, salt and any other seasonings; add the dissolved yeast and work the dough thoroughly together. An electric mixer with a dough hook may also be used for 3 min. at low speed.*

*3. Add the rest of the flour, a little at a time, and continue to knead the dough with your hands. The butter may be melted or rubbed into the last portion of flour before it is kneaded into the dough.*

*4. Remove the dough to a floured board. Knead it by pushing it away from you with the heels of your hands, gathering it back, turning it and repeating this motion. Repeat until the dough is firm and not sticky.*

*5. Make the flexible dough into a ball and put it into a bowl. Sprinkle a thin layer of flour on top. Cover with a clean cloth or plastic, and put the dough in a draft-free but not too warm place until it has doubled in bulk. The rising time depends on the kind of flour used, on the temperature of the liquid, and whether there is fat in the dough.*

*6. Remove the dough to a floured surface and press it flat with your hands. Knead lightly and form it into the shape you want. Place it in a tin or on a greased baking sheet and leave it to rise again in a draft-free place, at room temperature, until well risen. Brush the top, score it, and bake according to the recipe.*

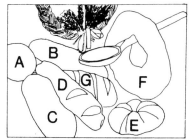

A. Round Caraway Seed Bread (page 17)
B. Bran Bread (below)
C. Whole-wheat Bread (page 18)
D. Farmer's Bread (page 17)
E. Coarse Round Bread (page 16)
F. Rye Flour Ring (page 16)
G. White Bread (page 12)

# Whole-wheat Breads

*The coarser types of bread contain important nutrients and fibers necessary for good health.*

### Bran Bread
(makes 2 loaves)
Preparation time: 15–20 min.
Rising time: about 1 hr.
Baking time: about 40 min.
Oven temperature: 400°
Lowest rack in the oven
Suitable for freezing

*3 oz. yeast*
*2 c. lukewarm water*
*1 tbsp. salt*
*$\frac{3}{4}$ c. wheat bran*
*4–$4\frac{1}{2}$ c. rye flour*
*3–$3\frac{1}{2}$ c. all-purpose flour*

1. Dissolve the yeast in lukewarm water and add to most of the wheat bran, rye flour and a little of the all-purpose flour. Add salt. Knead well and add more white flour, as needed.
2. Let the dough stand, covered, in a warm place to rise for about 40 min. Knead the dough lightly and add more flour, if necessary. Divide the dough in two and let it rest for 5–10 min. Form it into oblong loaves.
3. Leave the loaves to rise again on the baking sheet for about 20 min. Brush them with water, milk, cream or melted butter and sprinkle the rest of the wheat bran on top.
4. Bake the loaves as directed, and cool on a wire rack.

*Linseed Bread*

*Coarse Round Bread*

*Farmer's Bread*

When you have brushed the bread, score it before putting it in the oven. By doing this some of the carbon dioxide collected in the bread escapes during baking and prevents cracking.

Use a sharp knife, dip it in flour and lightly score the top. Above are different ways of scoring bread.

## Linseed Bread

(makes 2 loaves)
Preparation time: 15–20 min.
Rising time: about 2 hr.
Oven temperature: 425°
Middle rack in the oven
Suitable for freezing

3 oz. yeast
$2\frac{1}{2}$ c. lukewarm water
8–9 c. rye flour
1 tbsp. salt
3 tbsp. linseed
2 tbsp. caraway seeds
$2$–$2\frac{1}{2}$ c. all-purpose flour

1. Dissolve the yeast in $\frac{1}{2}$ c. lukewarm water, add remaining water, most of the rye flour, salt, linseed and caraway seeds. Knead the dough until it becomes elastic, adding the rest of the rye flour and as much all-purpose flour as necessary to prevent the dough from sticking to the bowl.
2. Place the dough, covered, in a warm place and let it rise for about $1\frac{1}{2}$ hr. Knead and form it into two round loaves which are then scored in a diamond pattern. Let these rise again for about 20–30 min. on a baking sheet, then brush with water.
3. Place a pan with water in the bottom of the oven and put the loaves on the middle rack. If the loaves become too brown, the temperature should be lowered near the end of the baking time, or the loaves covered with waxed paper or foil.
4. Brush the baked loaves with lukewarm water and cool on a wire rack with a cloth on top.

## Rye Flour Rings

(makes 2 rings)
Preparation time: 15–20 min.
Rising time: about 1 hr.
Baking time: about 50 min.
Oven temperature: 400°
Lowest rack in the oven
Suitable for freezing

$\frac{1}{4}$ c. butter
2 c. lukewarm water
2 oz. yeast
1 tbsp. salt
4–$4\frac{1}{2}$ c. fine whole-grain rye flour
2–$2\frac{1}{2}$ c. rye flour
2–$2\frac{1}{2}$ c. all-purpose flour

1. Melt the butter in the lukewarm water and dissolve the yeast in the mixture. Add salt, fine whole-grain rye flour and rye flour and knead the dough well. Add enough all-purpose flour for a firm, elastic consistency.
2. Divide the dough into two portions, roll them out into "sausages," and make a ring out of each. Lay them on the baking sheet, cover with a cloth, and let them rise for about 1 hr. in a warm place. (The rings only need to rise once.)
3. Brush the rings with water, sprinkle a little rye flour over them and bake as directed. Cool on a wire rack under a cloth.

## Coarse Round Bread

(makes 2 loaves)
Preparation time: 20 min. + 2 hr. for soaking the whole wheat
Rising time: about $1\frac{1}{4}$ hr.
Baking time: about 40 min.
Oven temperature: 400°
Lowest rack in the oven
Suitable for freezing

3 oz. crushed whole wheat grains
$\frac{1}{4}$ c. butter
2 c. skimmed milk
$\frac{1}{2}$ c. cottage cheese
2 oz. yeast
1 tbsp. salt
3–$3\frac{1}{2}$ c. rye flour
5–6 c. all-purpose flour

1. Pour hot water over the crushed wheat grains and let them soak for 2 hr. The water must not be boiling.
2. Melt the butter, add the milk, and be sure that the mixture is not warmer than 100°. Stir in the cottage cheese and pour a little of the mixture over the crumbled yeast.
3. Add salt, the drained crushed wheat, the remaining liquid and the rye flour, and stir well. Knead the dough with all-purpose flour until it becomes elastic and no longer sticks to the bowl. Cover, store in a warm place, and let it rise for about 50 min.
4. Divide the dough into two and let both parts rest for about 5 min. Make a ball out of each lump of dough, flatten it and place it on the baking sheet to rise for about 20 min. Brush with milk, cream, or melted

butter and cut a star with a sharp knife (cut deepest in the middle). Bake the round loaves as directed and cool them on a wire rack.

## Round Caraway Seed Bread

(makes 2 loaves)
Preparation time: about 20 min.
Rising time: about 1 hr.
Baking time: 35–40 min.
Oven temperature: 400°
Lowest rack in the oven
Suitable for freezing

2 oz. yeast
2 c. buttermilk
$\frac{1}{2}$ c. lukewarm water
1 tbsp. salt
4–5 tbsp. crushed whole-wheat grains
4–5 c. rye flour
3–3$\frac{1}{2}$ c. all-purpose flour

1. Dissolve the yeast in the lukewarm water and add the buttermilk (at room temperature), salt, the crushed whole wheat grains and most of the rye flour. Knead the dough thoroughly and add the rest of the rye flour. Knead the dough again with as much of the all-purpose flour as needed to make it elastic.
2. Let the dough stand covered in a warm place for about 40 min. Knead lightly and form it into two rounded loaves. Leave them to rise on a baking sheet for about 20 min.
3. Cut a slash across the loaves and brush them with milk, cream, or melted butter before baking as directed. Place the loaves on wire rack until they are cool.

## Farmer's Bread

(makes 2 loaves)
Preparation time: 20 min.
Rising time: about 1$\frac{1}{4}$ hr.
Baking time: about 30 min.
Oven temperature: 425°
Lowest rack in the oven
Suitable for freezing

2 oz. yeast
$\frac{3}{4}$ c. lukewarm water
1$\frac{1}{2}$ c. buttermilk
1 tbsp. salt
$\frac{1}{2}$ c. coarse rye flour
2–2$\frac{1}{2}$ c. whole-wheat flour

*Linseed Bread – is extremely healthy, and tasty too.*

2–2$\frac{1}{2}$ c. rye flour
3–4 c. all-purpose flour

1. Dissolve the yeast in the lukewarm water and add lukewarm buttermilk, salt, rye flours and whole-wheat flour. Knead the dough well and add enough all-purpose flour so that it no longer sticks to the bowl.
2. Let the dough stand, covered, in a warm place for about 45 min. Divide it in two and let the two portions rest for 3–4 min. Roll them out to two oblong loaves and let them rise again on the baking sheet for about 30 min.
3. Brush the loaves with coffee, milk, or cream. Cut diagonal slashes across their tops and bake as directed. Place on a wire rack until cool.

**Whole-wheat Bread** (2 loaves)
Preparation time: 20 min. + 2 hr.
for soaking the whole grain
Rising time: about 1¼ hr.
Baking time: about 40 min.
Oven temperature: 400–425°

Lowest rack in the oven
Suitable for freezing

6 tbsp. whole-wheat grains
3 oz. yeast
2 c. water
1 tbsp. salt
2 tbsp. melted butter
3–4 c. stone-ground whole-wheat flour
4–4½ c. all-purpose flour

1. Pour warm water over the whole grain and let stand for 2 hr. The water must not be boiling.
2. Dissolve the yeast in ½ c. lukewarm water. Add the remaining water, the melted butter, the wholewheat flour, the drained whole grains, and salt. Stir until the dough is elastic and add as much all-purpose flour as needed.
3. Let the dough stand, covered, in a warm place for about 45 min. Take it out of the bowl and divide it into two portions. Let them stand for a few minutes. Flatten them and roll them loosely together diagonally into two oblong loaves. Let them rise for about 20–25 min. on a baking sheet.
4. Sprinkle a little flour on the loaves and bake them as directed. Put a cloth over them when they have finished baking and cool on a wire rack.

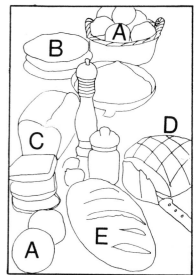

*What should a loaf of bread look like?*
*Loaves don't all have to be oblong, just look at the selection shown here:*
*A. Crusty Rolls*
*B. Coriander Bread (page 33)*
*C. Health Bread*
*D. Ham Bread*
*E. Yogurt Bread*

## Crusty Rolls

(makes 18–20 rolls)
Preparation time: about 20 min.
Rising time: about $\frac{3}{4}$ hr.
Baking time: about 15 min.
Oven temperature: 425°
Middle rack in the oven
Suitable for freezing

4–5 c. all-purpose flour
2 oz. yeast
1$\frac{1}{2}$–2 c. lukewarm water
2 tsp. salt
$\frac{1}{2}$ tsp. sugar
1 egg for brushing
poppy or sesame seeds

1. Sift the flour and put yeast in a hollow in the middle. Dissolve the yeast, adding $\frac{1}{2}$ c. lukewarm milk and add a little of the flour. Cover and leave in a warm place for about 15 min.
2. Add salt, sugar and lukewarm milk until the dough can be kneaded smooth and elastic, and let it stand for a further 15 min.
3. Remove the dough to a floured board, knead it and form 18–20 rolls. Leave these to rise again on a greased baking sheet for 15–20 min.
4. Brush the rolls with beaten egg and cut a slash in half of them with a thin, sharp knife. Sprinkle these rolls with poppy seeds and the others with sesame seeds. Put a saucer or a pan holding warm water in the bottom of the oven and bake the rolls for about 15 min. at 425°. Cool on a wire rack.

## Ham Bread

(makes 1 large loaf)
Preparation time: 20 min.
Rising time: about 1 hr.
Baking time: about 40 min.
Oven temperature: 425°
Lowest rack in the oven
Suitable for freezing

$\frac{1}{4}$ c. butter or margarine
$\frac{1}{2}$ c. milk
2 oz. yeast
1 tsp. salt
$\frac{1}{2}$ tsp. ground aniseed and fennel, mixed
2 onions
1 clove garlic
$\frac{1}{4}$ lb. cooked ham
1 c. stone-ground whole-wheat flour
2–3 c. all-purpose flour

1. Melt butter or margarine, add milk and keep the mixture lukewarm. Dissolve the yeast in a little of the mixture and add the remaining milk, together with the eggs, salt, aniseed, fennel and stone-ground flour. Stir until well mixed.
2. Chop onions very finely and mix them with crushed garlic, the coarsely minced ham and about $\frac{1}{2}$ c. all-purpose flour. Stir into the dough.
3. Knead the dough thoroughly and add more flour until it is elastic. Cover the dough and leave in a warm place for about 40 min.
4. Remove the dough to a floured board and form a round loaf. Let the bread rise again for about 20 min., slash lightly in a diamond pattern and brush with water or milk. The bread can be sprinkled with 2–3 tbsp. stone-ground flour, mixed with a little coarse sea salt, aniseed and fennel. Bake for 40 min. at 425° and cool on a rack.

## Yogurt Bread

(makes 2 loaves)
Preparation time: 15 min.
Rising time: about 1 hr.
Baking time: about 30 min.
Oven temperature: 400°
Lowest rack in the oven
Suitable for freezing

6 tbsp. crushed whole-wheat grains or $\frac{1}{2}$ c. stone-ground whole-wheat flour
2 c. water
3 oz. yeast
1 tbsp. salt
1 tbsp. linseed (optional)
$\frac{3}{4}$ c. natural plain yogurt
1$\frac{1}{2}$–2 c. wholemeal flour
4–4$\frac{1}{2}$ c. all-purpose flour

1. Pour about $\frac{3}{4}$ c. boiling water over the crushed wheat grains or the stone-ground wheat flour and let stand until lukewarm. Dissolve the yeast in the remaining water, also lukewarm, and add the wheat grains, linseed and yogurt – all at room temperature.
2. Stir the whole-wheat flour mixed with about half the all-purpose flour and salt. Combine thoroughly with a wooden spoon or mix for 3–4 min. in a food mixer with a dough hook. Add more all-purpose flour and work the dough with your hands until it is smooth and elastic. Cover and store in a warm place to rise for about 40 min.
3. Remove the dough from the bowl and place on a floured board. Knead it lightly, form two portions and let stand for 5 min. Pat or roll out until they are flat, fold over in the middle making an oval shape, and slash top (see illustration, page 18). Leave to rise again on a greased baking sheet for about 20 min.
4. Brush the loaves with water, milk or melted butter and sprinkle top with wheat grains or stone-ground wheat. Bake for 30 min. at 400° and cool on a wire rack.

## Health Bread

(makes 1 loaf)
Preparation time: about 15 min.
Rising time: about 1$\frac{1}{4}$ hr.
Baking time: 35–40 min.
Oven temperature: 400°
Lowest rack in the oven
Suitable for freezing

2 oz. yeast
$\frac{3}{4}$ c. lukewarm water
1 c. buttermilk
1 tbsp. oil
1 c. wheat bran
2 tsp. salt
1–1$\frac{1}{4}$ c. stone-ground whole-wheat flour
4–5 c. all-purpose flour

1. Dissolve the yeast in the lukewarm water and add lukewarm milk, oil, wheat bran, salt, and whole-wheat flour. Let the mixture stand for about 15 min.
2. Add all-purpose flour, a little at a time, and knead the dough thoroughly. Cover and place in a warm place to rise for about 40 min.
3. Remove the dough and place on a floured board, knead it lightly and form into an oblong loaf. Put into a greased baking tin and set aside to rise in a warm place for about 20 min. Cut a slash lengthwise, brush with water and sprinkle a little wheat bran on top. Bake for 35–40 min. at 400° and cool the bread on a wire rack. For a soft crust, place a clean cloth over the bread while cooling.

19

# Good Old-fashioned Breads

## Spiced Bread
(makes 2 loaves)
Preparation time: 15–20 min.
Rising time: 50–60 min.
Baking time: about 30 min.
Oven temperature: 400–425°
Lowest rack in the oven
Suitable for freezing

4–5 c. all-purpose flour
2 oz. yeast
1 c. lukewarm milk
$\frac{1}{4}$ c. butter or margarine
2 eggs
2 tsp. salt
$\frac{1}{2}$ tsp. pepper
1 tbsp. caraway seeds
1–2 tsp. coriander (optional)

1. Sift flour, salt and pepper and make a hollow in the center. Put in the yeast, and the lukewarm milk and dissolve the yeast in the milk with a little of the flour. Cover and let stand for 15 min.
2. Add softened butter, 1 egg, $\frac{1}{2}$ tbsp. caraway seeds and $\frac{1}{2}$ tsp. ground coriander. Knead the dough thoroughly. Cover and leave to rise in a warm place for around 20 min.
3. Remove dough to a floured board and divide it into two. Let the portions rest for 3–4 min., then shape into two oblong loaves. Let these rise again on a baking sheet for around 20 min.
4. Slash, brush with beaten egg and sprinkle remaining caraway seeds and coriander over the top. Bake as directed, then cool under a clean cloth on a wire rack.

## Malt Bread
(makes 1 loaf)
Preparation time: about 15 min.
Rising time: about 2 hr.
Baking time: about 1 hr.
Oven temperature: 400°
Lowest rack in the oven
Suitable for freezing

3–$3\frac{1}{2}$ c. all-purpose flour
3–$3\frac{1}{2}$ c. rye flour
6 tbsp. sugar
1 tsp. salt
$1\frac{1}{2}$ oz. yeast
$1\frac{1}{2}$ c. lukewarm milk

$\frac{1}{2}$ c. malt beer
1 tbsp. maple syrup
$\frac{1}{2}$ tsp. ground ginger
2 oz. raisins

1. Mix most of the flour with the sugar and salt. Dissolve the yeast in a little lukewarm milk and beer. Add to the flour together with the remaining liquid, mix to a dough and let it rise for $\frac{1}{2}$–1 hr.
2. Mix in syrup and remaining flour mixed with the ginger and the raisins. Let the dough rise again for about $\frac{1}{2}$ hr. Form into a round or oblong loaf, and let it rise on a baking sheet for about 15 min. Brush with sugared water and bake as directed.

This is an especially heavy and sweet dough, and therefore is made first as an ordinary dough without syrup. When the fermentation is well under way, the syrup is added together with the rest of the flour. Very sweet, heavy doughs should be made in this way.

## French Country Bread
(makes 2 loaves)
Preparation time: about 20 min.
Rising time: about 3 hr.
Baking time: about 40 min.
Oven temperature: 475 and 325°
Lowest rack in the oven
Suitable for freezing

1 oz. yeast
2 c. lukewarm water
1 tbsp. salt
2 tbsp. oil
8–9 c. all-purpose flour

1. Dissolve the yeast in the lukewarm water. Add oil, salt and at least half the flour. Mix the dough thoroughly with a wooden spoon and knead in the rest of the flour. Cover the dough and store in a warm place to rise for about 2 hr. at room temperature.
2. Remove the dough to a floured board and knead it lightly. Divide into two and let the portions rest for about 5 min. Roll out as two oblong loaves, cover them and place on a baking sheet to rise again for about 1 hr.
3. Cut diagonal slashes, brush with water and sprinkle a little flour on top. Bake for 15–20 min. at 475°, then reduce the heat to 325° and bake for the remainder of the time. Place the loaves on a wire rack to cool.

## Rolls with Herb Flavoring
(makes 25 rolls)
Preparation time: about 20 min.
Rising time: about 50 min.
Baking time: about 12–15 min.
Oven temperature: 425–450°
Middle rack in the oven
Suitable for freezing

1 oz. yeast
$1\frac{1}{4}$ c. lukewarm milk
4–$4\frac{1}{2}$ c. all-purpose flour
$\frac{1}{4}$ c. butter or margarine
2 eggs
2 tsp. salt
$\frac{1}{2}$ tsp. nutmeg
4 tbsp. chopped fresh herbs (chives, dill, parsley, etc.)

1. Dissolve the yeast in about $\frac{1}{2}$ c. lukewarm milk, stir in half the flour and set the dough aside to rise for 15 min.
2. Add softened butter, 1 egg, salt, the remaining milk, nutmeg and the chopped fresh herbs (chives, dill, parsley, etc.). Knead the rest of the flour into the dough until it is elastic. Place in a warm place to rise for about 20 min.
3. Remove the dough to a floured board and cut it into small portions to make rolls. Roll them out and let them rise again on a greased sheet for 15–20 min.
4. Cut a slit in each small roll with a sharp knife, brush with beaten egg and bake as directed. Place the rolls on a wire rack to cool.

*In the basket and on the table are delicious Rolls with Herb Flavoring. On the table is tasty Spiced Bread sprinkled with caraway seeds and coriander.*

# Bread made with Sourdough

*The baking of this type of bread must be planned well in advance, as the dough needs time to develop. But it needs very little attention and is no more difficult to work with than other yeast doughs. The advantage is that the loaves are moist and keep well.*

**Coarse Rye Bread with Sourdough**
(see photo, page 6)
(makes 2 loaves)
Preparation time: about 20 min.
Rising time: about 3 hr. +
24 hr. for the sourdough
Baking time: about 1 hr.
Oven temperature: 400°
Lowest rack in the oven
Suitable for freezing

**Sourdough:**
$\frac{1}{2}$ c. whole or crushed rye grains
$\frac{1}{2}$ c. water

$1\frac{3}{4}$ c. coarsely ground rye
1 c. buttermilk
**Dough:** 3 oz. yeast
1 c. lukewarm water
1 tbsp. salt
7–8 c. finely ground rye flour
$2\frac{1}{2}$–3 c. all-purpose flour

1. Pour $\frac{1}{2}$ c. boiling water over whole or crushed rye grains and let stand until the water is lukewarm. Add coarse rye flour and buttermilk and let the sourdough stand, covered, at room temperature for 24 hr.
2. Dissolve the yeast in the lukewarm water and stir in the sourdough. Add salt and finely ground rye flour and work the dough thoroughly. Knead in the all-purpose flour until the dough is firm and smooth. Set it aside to rise at room temperature for about 2 hr.
3. Knead the dough well and divide it into two. Form loaves and place them in greased baking tins. Let them rise for 1 hr. and brush them with water. Make a cut lengthwise and prick with a fork. Sprinkle whole rye grains on top and bake as directed. Place the loaves, covered, on a wire rack to cool. Wait a day before you slice the bread.

**Rye Bread with Cottage Cheese and Sourdough**
(makes 1 loaf)
Preparation time: about 20 min.
Rising time: about $1\frac{1}{4}$ hr. +
24 hr. for sourdough
Baking time: about 40–45 min.
Oven temperature: 400°
Lowest rack in the oven
Suitable for freezing

**Sourdough:**
1 c. coarsely ground rye flour
$\frac{3}{4}$ c. cottage cheese
**Dough:** 2 oz. yeast
1 c. lukewarm water
$1\frac{3}{4}$ c. rye flour
3 tsp. salt
$2\frac{1}{2}$–3 c. all-purpose flour

1. Stir together the coarse rye flour and the cottage cheese, cover and set aside for 24 hr. at room temperature or a little cooler (not in the refrigerator).
2. Stir the sourdough and yeast in the lukewarm water and add rye flour, salt, and most of the all-purpose flour. Mix the dough thoroughly with the remaining flour, as needed. Let it stand to rise in a warm place for 45 min.

*Below: Two good breads made with sourdough, and which keep well – Rye Bread with Cottage Cheese, and Graham Bread.*

3. Knead the dough, form it into a round loaf and let it rise again for 30 min. on a baking sheet.
4. Cut slashes or prick with a fork, brush with water and sprinkle a little flour on top. Bake as directed and cool on a wire rack.

## Graham Bread with Sourdough
(makes 1 loaf)
Preparation time: 15–20 min.
Rising time: about 1½ hr. + 24 hr. for sourdough
Baking time: about 35–40 min.
Oven temperature: 400°
Lowest rack in the oven
Suitable for freezing

### Sourdough:
*1 c. buttermilk*
*1¾ c. wholemeal flour*
**Dough:** *2 oz. yeast*
*¾ c. lukewarm water*
*2–3 tsp. salt*
*1 tbsp. oil*
*1¾ c. wholemeal flour*
*2½–3 c. all-purpose flour*

1. Stir the flour and buttermilk together to make the sourdough, cover and let stand at room temperature for 24 hr.
2. Dissolve the sourdough in the lukewarm water together with the yeast and add salt, oil and then the wholemeal flour. Work the dough thoroughly and knead in the all-purpose flour. Cover and set aside to rise for about 1 hr.
3. Knead the dough on a floured board and form it into a large loaf. Set aside to rise on a baking sheet for about 30 min. Cut diagonal slashes, brush with water, and sprinkle a little flour on top. Bake as directed and leave the bread, covered, on a wire rack to cool.

## Rye Bread with Sourdough
(makes 2 loaves)
Preparation time: about 15–20 min.
Rising time: about 1½ hr. + 48 hr. for the sourdough
Baking time: about 1¼ hr.
Oven temperature: 400°
Lowest rack in the oven
Suitable for freezing

### Sourdough:
*1 c. rye flour*
*½ c. buttermilk*
*½ tsp. salt*
**Dough:** *2 oz. yeast*

*2 c. lukewarm water*
*3 tsp. salt*
*4–4½ c. rye flour*
*2½–3 c. all-purpose flour*

1. Mix together the 1 c. rye flour, buttermilk and salt, cover and set aside at room temperature for 48 hr.
2. Dissolve the sourdough in the lukewarm water together with the yeast. Add salt and rye flour, mix dough well and knead it with the all-purpose flour until elastic. Cover and put in a warm place to rise for about 1 hr.
3. Knead the dough on a floured board and divide it into two pieces. Form oblong loaves. Put them beside each other, with greased foil between, in a small roasting pan or ovenproof dish. Let them rise again for about 30 min.
4. Brush with water, prick with a fork and bake as directed.

Turn the loaves out onto a wire rack and cool a little before you separate them. Cover with a cloth. Wait 24 hr. before you slice the bread.

*Below: Rye Bread with Sourdough is good with salami.*

# Wholesome Breads

## Dark Country Bread

(makes 2 loaves)
Preparation time: about 15–20 min.
Rising time: about 2 hr.
Baking time: about 40 min.
Oven temperature: 400°
Lowest rack in the oven
Suitable for freezing

1 oz. yeast
2 c. lukewarm water
3 tsp. salt
3 tbsp. oil
1½ c. rye flour
2 c. wholemeal flour
3–4 c. all-purpose flour

1. Dissolve the yeast in the lukewarm water and add salt, oil, rye flour and wholemeal flour. Mix the dough smoothly until elastic and add all-purpose flour until the dough is sufficiently firm. Cover and let stand in a warm place to rise for about 1½ hr.
2. Remove the dough to a floured board and divide it into two. Form into two oblong loaves and put them on a baking sheet to rise for about 30 min. Brush with water, prick well with a fork or slash. Let the loaves cool on a wire rack with, if you want a soft crust, a cloth on top.

VARIATION

For a coarser bread, use coarsely ground rye flour instead of ordinary rye flour.

## Rye Bread

(makes 2 loaves)
Preparation time: about 15–20 min.
Rising time: about 1 hr. 20–25 min.
Baking time: about 35–40 min.
Oven temperature: 400°
Lowest rack in the oven
Suitable for freezing

2 oz. yeast
¾ c. lukewarm water
1 tbsp. salt
1½ c. buttermilk
3 tbsp. oil
3½ c. rye flour
4–4½ c. all-purpose flour

1. Dissolve the yeast in the lukewarm water and add buttermilk (at room temperature), oil and rye flour. Mix the dough thoroughly and add salt and as much all-purpose flour as necessary. Cover, and set aside in a warm place to rise for about 1 hr.
2. Knead the dough lightly and divide into two. Form round or oblong loaves, cover and place on a baking sheet for 20–25 min. to rise again. Brush the loaves with milk, cream or beaten egg. Cut diagonal slashes on oblong loaves and a diamond pattern, with ¾–1 in. spaces, on round loaves (see page 16). Bake as directed and cool on a wire rack.

VARIATION

Rye bread can be baked with equal parts of rye flour and strong plain flour if you want a firmer bread. If 1–2 tbsp. caraway seeds are added, the bread will have an interesting flavor.

## Basket Bread

(makes 2 loaves)
Preparation time: about 20 min.
Rising time: about 1 hr.
Baking time: about 30 min.
Oven temperature: 400°
Lowest rack in the oven
Suitable for freezing

2 oz. yeast
1½ c. lukewarm water
3 tsp. salt
¾ c. natural plain yogurt
2¼ c. whole-wheat flour
3 c. rye flour
2¾–3 c. all-purpose flour

1. Dissolve the yeast in the lukewarm water and add the yogurt, which should be at room temperature. Add salt, rye flour and whole-wheat flour, and mix thoroughly with a wooden spoon or a fork until elastic. Knead in all-purpose flour and put the dough, covered, in a warm place to rise for 30–40 min.
2. Knead the dough on a floured board and divide it into two. Form into round loaves and put them into greased and flour-sprinkled baskets. Cover, and leave to rise again for about 30 min.
3. Turn the loaves out carefully onto a baking sheet and bake as directed. Brush the baked loaves with lukewarm water, sprinkle with a little flour, and put on a wire rack to cool.

# Bread Baked in a Pan or Mold

**Herb Bread** (left)
(makes 2 loaves)
Mold: 4-inch clay flower-pots
Preparation time: about 25 min.
Rising time: about 50 min.
Baking time: about 40 min.
Oven temperature: 425°
Lowest rack in the oven
Suitable for freezing

*4–4½ c. all-purpose flour*
*2 oz. yeast*
*½ c. lukewarm milk*
*2 tsp. salt*
*½ tsp. sugar*
*¼ c. butter or margarine*
*2 eggs*
*4 tbsp. chopped fresh dill*
*1–2 tsp. dried fennel*
*½ tsp. dried rosemary*
*pinch of nutmeg*
*1–2 tsp. aniseed*

1. Sift the flour and make a hollow in the center. Put in the yeast, pour lukewarm milk (at about 100°) over it and dissolve the yeast with sugar and a little of the flour. Cover the bowl and leave in a warm place for 15 min. for the dough to rise.
2. Stir melted, slightly cooled butter with the lightly beaten egg, salt, finely chopped fresh dill, herbs and nutmeg. Keep a little of the aniseed for decoration.
3. Pour the mixture into the bowl with the dough and mix thoroughly. Cover and set aside in a warm place for about 15 min. to rise.
4. Remove the dough to a floured board, divide it into two and put into flower-pots which have been washed, dried, and brushed with oil. Put in large plastic bags and set aside to rise for about 20 min. Brush with water and sprinkle the rest of the aniseed on top. Bake at 425° for about 40 min. Turn the loaves out carefully onto a wire rack to cool. They can be put back into the flower-pots when they are to be served.

Herb bread can be frozen with or without the flower-pots, but clay flower-pots easily break if jolted in the freezer. They must therefore be well protected and should be wrapped in foil.

**White Pan Loaf** (above)
(makes 2 loaves)
2 2-lb. loaf pans
Preparation time: about 15–20 min.
Rising time: about 50 min.
Baking time: about 30–40 min.
Oven temperature: 425°
Lowest rack in the oven
Suitable for freezing

*¼ c. butter or margarine*
*2 c. skimmed milk*
*2 oz. yeast*
*½ tbsp. salt*
*½–1 tsp. sugar*
*8–9 c. all-purpose flour*
*egg or cream for brushing*

1. Melt butter or margarine and add the milk, making sure that the mixture does not get warmer than 100°. Dissolve the yeast in about ½ c. of this liquid and add sugar.
2. Stir in the remaining liquid alternately with at least half the flour and salt. Mix the dough thoroughly with a wooden spoon or for 3–4 min. in a food mixer with a dough hook. Knead in the rest of the flour with your hands, cover and put in a warm place to rise for about 30 min.
3. Remove the dough to a floured board and divide it into two. Shape into two large "buns" and let them stand 4–5 min. Roll out or flatten the "buns" into thick slabs, fold the sides in toward the middle and fold them again lengthwise into oblong loaves. Put them into greased pans. Brush with egg or cream.
4. Bake the loaves at 425° for 30–40 min. Take them out of the pan for the last 10 min. if the bottom and sides are not brown enough. Place them on their sides and turn them after 5 min. Cool on a wire rack. You can also make French Bread from this recipe. Roll out two long portions, score 3–4 times diagonally with a sharp knife, brush with cream or egg and bake for about 30 min. at 400°.

# Additions to Vary the Flavor

*Bread may be varied to suit your taste and the occasion. The following recipes use a neutral basic recipe as a starting point and add spices, onion, cheese, tomatoes, mushrooms, bacon, olives, and salami. You will find them interesting to bake as well as to eat.*

### Basic Dough
(makes 2–4 loaves depending on size)
Preparation time: about 20 min.
Rising time: about 1 hr.
Baking time: 35–45 min.
Oven temperature: 400–425°
Lowest rack in the oven
Suitable for freezing

2 oz. yeast
$2\frac{1}{2}$ c. lukewarm water
2–3 tsp. salt
$2–2\frac{1}{4}$ c. rye flour
6–7 c. all-purpose flour

1. Dissolve the yeast in $\frac{1}{2}$–$\frac{3}{4}$ c. lukewarm water. Add salt, the remaining water, the rye flour and half of the all-purpose flour. Stir the dough thoroughly and knead in the rest of the all-purpose flour with the hands until elastic. Cover and put in a warm place to rise for about 30 min.
2. Remove the dough to a floured board and knead it slightly. Add the flavor ingredients (see individual recipes). Divide the dough, form into loaves and set aside to rise again for 30 min. Bake according to recipes.

### Onion Bread (left)
(makes 2 loaves)
Preparation time, Rising time and Baking time: see Basic Dough (page 28)

$\frac{1}{2}$ quantity Basic Dough
3–4 onions
$\frac{1}{2}$ tsp. pepper
2 tbsp. butter or margarine
cream for brushing top

1. Set aside the dough to rise. Meanwhile, clean and roughly chop the onions. Sauté them in butter on low heat for 5 min., then cool.

2. Knead the dough with the onion, pepper and a little more flour until it is elastic and does not stick to the board. Form two long thin loaves and set them aside to rise, covered, on a greased baking sheet, for 25–30 min.
3. Cut diagonal slashes with a sharp knife, brush with cream and sprinkle a little flour on top. Bake for 30–35 min. at 425° and cool on a wire rack.

Serve Onion Bread cut in slices, with soup and other supper dishes. It is also good with butter only and for any kind of sandwich.

**Cheese Bread** (right)
(makes 1 loaf)
Preparation time, Rising time and Baking time: see Basic Dough (page 28)

$\frac{1}{2}$ *quantity Basic Dough*
*5 oz. Cheddar cheese*
*1 small onion*
*cream for brushing top*

1. Set the dough to rise. Meanwhile grate the cheese coarsely. Chop the onion finely.
2. Remove the dough to a floured board and knead in the cheese and onion together with a little more flour. Form the dough into a round loaf, put it on a greased baking sheet and let it rise again under a cloth or plastic wrap for about 30 min.
3. Brush the bread with cream, sprinkle a thin layer of flour over the top and bake at 400° for about 45 min. Place the bread on a rack to cool.

*Cheese Bread (right) is delicious with soups, casseroles, vegetable dishes, and salads.*

## Pizza Bread

(makes 1 loaf)
1 2-lb. loaf tin
Preparation time, Rising time and
Baking time: see Basic Dough (page
28)

½ quantity Basic Dough
2 tbsp. butter or margarine
1 onion
½ lb. raw chopped meat
10 stuffed olives (optional)
3 small tomatoes
salt, pepper
paprika
marjoram
oregano
basil

1. Set the dough aside to rise.
2. Brown the finely chopped onion
and the meat lightly in the butter
and add chopped stuffed olives. Scald
and skin the tomatoes, cut them into
four and squeeze out the seeds.
Roughly chop the tomatoes and put
into the saucepan together with the
onion and the meat.
3. Cook the mixture until all liquid
has evaporated. Season with the fresh
or dried herbs and spices.
4. Roll out the dough fairly thin but
with one side equal in length to a 2
lb. loaf tin. Spread the filling on the
dough, moisten the edges with water
and roll up starting with one of the
long sides, like a jelly roll. Place in
a greased tin, cover and let stand for
about 20 min. to rise. Brush top with
water, sprinkle with a thin layer of
flour and bake for about 45 min. at
400°. Cool on a wire rack.

## Bacon Bread

(makes 1 loaf)
Preparation time, Rising time and
Baking time: see Basic Dough (page
28)

½ quantity Basic Dough
¼ lb. lean bacon
1 leek
1 small onion
¼ lb. mushrooms
dill
1 tbsp. chopped chives
1 tbsp. chopped parsley
salt
whole peppercorns
coriander seeds

1. Set the dough aside to rise.
2. Meanwhile, roughly chop the
bacon and brown the pieces lightly

in a dry frying pan together with the
finely sliced leek, chopped onion, and
chopped mushrooms.
3. Drain off the bacon fat, mix the
finely chopped herbs with the veg-
etables and bacon and season to taste.
Knead the filling into the dough,
possibly adding a little more flour if
necessary.
4. Divide the dough into three portions. Roll each out to a long, thin
roll about 16 in. long and braid them
together. Fold the ends under. Leave
to rise again on the baking sheet for
about 20 min. Brush with water and
sprinkle with a little whole or crushed
peppercorns and coriander seeds.
Bake for about 45 min. at 400°. Place
the bread on a wire rack to cool.

## Salami Bread

(makes 1 loaf)
Preparation time, Rising time and
Baking time: see Basic Dough (page
28)

½ quantity Basic Dough
4 onions
5–7 oz. salami
2–3 oz. cheese
2 tbsp. finely chopped parsley
coarse sea salt

1. Put the dough aside to rise. Cut
onions, salami and cheese into small
cubes and knead them into the risen
dough together with the parsley and
possibly a little more flour. Add sea-
soning to taste.
2. Form the dough into a round,
rather flat loaf and put it aside to rise
again on a greased baking sheet. Cut
a diamond pattern as shown on page
16, brush with water and sprinkle
with sea salt mixed with 1 tbsp. flour.
3. Bake for about 45 min. at 400° and
cool the bread on a wire rack.

## Other Suggestions

Don't just rely on the recipes already
given for adding different ingredients. Be adventurous and think up
other combinations to give an interesting taste. Experiment with celery,
colorful red and green peppers, or
add all kinds of sausages to the same
basic dough. There are so many other
kinds of herbs and spices to try, too.

*From left to right: Bacon Bread with
bacon, leek, onion and mushrooms;
Salami Bread with onion and cheese;
Pizza Bread*

# Exciting Breads

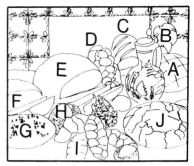

A. Linseed Bread (page 16), B. and D. Braided breads, C. Onion Bread (page 28), E. Cheese Bread (page 29), F. Graham Bread (page 10), G. Coriander Bread (below), H. Crusty Rolls (page 19), I. Braided Rolls (page 34), F. Rye Bread (page 25)

**Coriander Bread**
(makes 5–6 loaves)
Preparation time: about 20 min.
Rising time: about 45 min.
Baking time: about 20 min.
Oven temperature: 425°
Middle rack in the oven
Suitable for freezing

2 oz. yeast
1 c. lukewarm skimmed milk
2 tsp. salt
$\frac{1}{2}$ tsp. honey
1 egg
1 tbsp. coriander
1 tbsp. linseed
$\frac{1}{2}$ tsp. aniseed
2–2$\frac{1}{4}$ c. rye flour
3–3$\frac{1}{2}$ c. all-purpose flour

1. Dissolve the yeast in the luke-warm milk and add honey, egg and a coarsely ground mixture of coriander, linseed and aniseed. Stir in the salt and the rye flour until the dough is elastic. Then knead in the plain flour with your hands.
2. Let the dough rise in a warm place, covered, for about 30 min. Remove to a floured board and divide into five or six portions. Form these into "buns" and roll them flat. Let them rise again for about 15 min. on a baking sheet.
3. Brush the loaves with water and sprinkle whole or crushed coriander seeds and a little flour on top. Bake for 20 min. at 425° and cool on a wire rack. Coriander Bread is excellent with soups and other supper dishes.

# Dinner Rolls

*Small rolls are a welcome addition to a dinner party. It is easy and economical to make these rolls yourself, and when you have tried once you will certainly want to do it more often. As with most yeast baking, small rolls are well suited for freezing, so it is worthwhile baking a large quantity.*

**Dinner Rolls with Cottage Cheese**
(makes 60–80 small rolls)
Preparation time: about 30 min.
Rising time: about 30–40 min.
Baking time: about 12–15 min.
Oven temperature: 425°
Middle rack in the oven
Suitable for freezing

$\frac{1}{4}$ c. butter or margarine
2 c. skimmed milk
1 c. cottage cheese
2 oz. yeast
$1\frac{1}{2}$–2 tsp. salt
5–5$\frac{1}{2}$ c. all-purpose flour
1 egg for brushing top
**Decoration:** whole-wheat grains, sesame seeds, poppy seeds, sea salt, or the equivalent

1. Melt the butter or margarine, add the milk and keep the mixture at under 100°. Crumble the yeast and dissolve it in 4–7 oz. of the liquid. Add the remaining milk, the cottage cheese and the salt. Thoroughly stir in half the flour.

2. Remove the dough to a floured board, add the remaining flour a little at a time and knead well. Flatten or roll out the dough and fold it together again. Repeat this several times. Put in a bowl, sprinkle with a thin layer of flour, cover, and put in a warm place. The dough will have finished rising when it has about doubled in size.

3. Remove to a floured board, divide it into four portions and roll each of them out to a long "sausage." Divide each into 15–20 pieces and shape into small round or oval rolls, mini loaves or braided bread. (See dia-

### Braided Rolls

*1. Form 14–16 rounds from $\frac{1}{4}$ quantity Basic Dough (see page 28) and divide each round into three.*
*2. Roll out into thin "sausages" and press together, three at one end.*
*3. Braid as shown and turn under the ends. Leave to rise again on a greased baking sheet for about 15 min.*
*4. Brush with egg and decorate. Bake as directed for Basic Dough.*

1

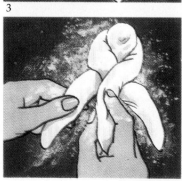

2

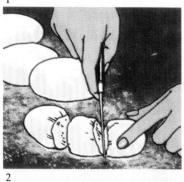

3

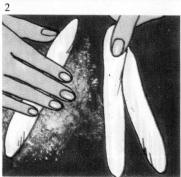

4

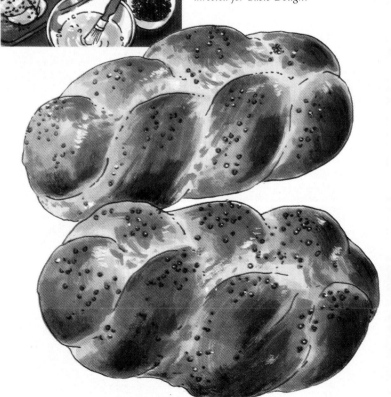

grams below for making Braided Rolls).

4. Leave to rise again on a greased baking sheet for 15–20 min. Make a cut in the round or oval rolls with a sharp knife, or clip a notch with sharp scissors.

5. Brush rolls or loaves with beaten egg and, if you like, sprinkle seeds or sea salt on top. Bake until they are golden in color. Cool them on a wire rack.

To freeze, pack them in foil before they are completely cool. Let them stand in the freezer wrappings until they are quite cool and then put them in the freezer. To thaw, heat them in the oven at 375–400° for a few minutes.

## Croissants (Crescent Rolls)

1. Roll out the dough to a square on a floured board.
2. Fold the dough in over the butter and roll out carefully.
3. Fold together, turn a quarter of the way around and roll out again. Repeat this three times.
4. Dip a knife in flour and cut each of the two round slabs into eight triangles.
5. Begin from the outside of the triangle and roll toward the tip. If you are afraid that the roll will come undone, you can brush the tip with a little water or egg. Bend into crescents, place them on a greased baking sheet to rise again. Brush with beaten egg and bake as explained in the recipe.

## Croissants (Crescent Rolls)

(makes 16 croissants)
Preparation time: about 30 min.
Rising time: about 5½ hr.
Baking time: about 15–20 min.
Oven temperature: 425°
Middle rack in the oven
Suitable for freezing

*1 oz. yeast*
*1 c. lukewarm milk*
*½–1 tsp. salt*
*¾ c. butter or margarine*
*4–5 c. all-purpose flour*
*1 egg for brushing top*

1. Dissolve yeast in the lukewarm milk. Mix to an elastic smooth dough with about 2 c. flour. Crumble almost ½ the butter in about 2 c. flour with the tips of the fingers. Sprinkle the butter and flour mixture into the yeast dough, and mix thoroughly with a wooden spoon. Add salt and more flour to make the dough smooth.

2. Cover and set the dough to rise in a cool place for 4–5 hr. or overnight.

3. Remove dough to a floured board, knead it well and roll it out to a square. Roll remaining chilled butter between two layers of plastic, remove the plastic and lay the butter in the middle of the dough. Fold the dough and gently roll it out until you can see the butter. Fold the dough together and cut and roll crescents as shown in the illustration.

4. Let the crescents rise again on a greased baking sheet, then bake for 15–20 min. at 425°. Cool on a wire rack.

1
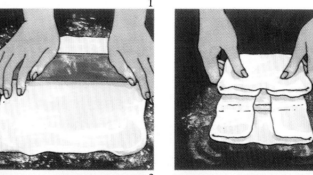
2

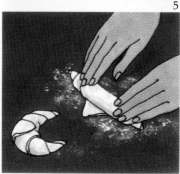
3
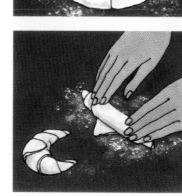
4

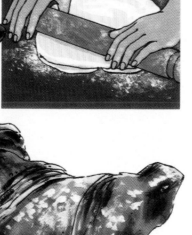

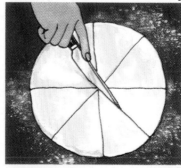
5

# One Dough, Many Loaves

*There are many ways to shape yeast dough. Here are a few examples, all baked with the same basic dough except for the genuine French bread.*

## Basic Dough

Preparation time: about 15 min.
Rising time: 1 hr. in all
Baking time: about 30 min.
Oven temperature: 400–425°
Lowest rack in the oven
Suitable for freezing

2 oz. yeast
$\frac{1}{2}$ c. lukewarm water
1 c. skim milk
1 tbsp. salt
2 tbsp. oil
$1\frac{3}{4}$ c. rye flour

$3\frac{1}{2}$–$4\frac{1}{2}$ c. all-purpose flour

1. Dissolve the yeast in the lukewarm water. Add lukewarm milk, salt, oil, rye flour and most of the all-purpose flour.
2. Mix the dough thoroughly and knead in the remaining flour by hand until the dough is elastic, even, and not too hard. Cover and put in a warm place to rise for about 35–40 min., until doubled in bulk.
3. Shape the dough and allow to rise again as explained in the individual recipes, and bake as directed above.

## Twisted Bread
(makes 1–2 loaves)

1. Remove the basic dough to a floured board and knead it lightly. Form into one large or two small, oblong loaves and twist them a couple of times.
2. Cover and let them rise again on a baking sheet for 20–25 min. Make a cut lengthwise with a sharp knife and brush them with water. Bake according to the basic recipe and cool on a wire rack.

## Round Wheat Bread
(makes 1 loaf)

1. Knead the basic dough lightly on a floured board after it has risen and form a large round loaf. Let this rise on a baking sheet for 20–25 min. under a cloth.
2. Cut a diamond pattern with a sharp knife, brush with water or milk, and bake according to the basic recipe. Cool the loaf on a wire rack.

## Wreaths
(makes 1–2 wreaths)

1. Knead the basic dough lightly on a floured board after it has finished rising. Roll out into two or four long "sausages." Twine these into one or two wreaths.
2. Let the wreaths rise again on a baking sheet for 20–25 min. Brush with water or milk. Bake thin wreaths for 20 min. at 425–450° and a thick wreath for 30–35 min. at 400°. Cool on a wire rack. Sprinkle the wreaths with poppy or sesame seeds before baking.

## Sesame Star
(makes 1 star)

1. Knead the risen dough lightly on a floured board. Make a large "bun" of about a fourth of the dough, and place it in the middle of a greased baking sheet. Divide the rest of the dough into six and form small round shapes, a little pointed at one end. Place them closely around the large "bun" with the points facing outward.
2. Let the star rise again for 20–25 min., covered. Make cuts to emphasize the star form (see illustration). Brush with milk, sprinkle sesame seeds on top and bake according to the basic recipe.

## Crescents with Poppy Seeds
(see photo, page 6)
(makes 16–24 crescents)

1. When the dough has finished rising, remove it to a floured board and knead it lightly. Roll out into two round slabs and cut each slab into 8–10 triangles. Roll them up, start-ing at the broad end and bending them a little.
2. Place the crescents, with the point down, on a greased baking sheet and let them rise again under a cloth for about 20 min. Brush with cream or beaten egg and sprinkle poppy seeds on top.

Bake for about 15 min. at 425–450° and cool on a wire rack.

## French Bread (Baguette)
(makes 3–4 loaves)
Preparation time: about 15–20 min.
Rising time: about 2½ hr.
Baking time: about 12–15 min.
Oven temperature: 475–500°
Middle rack in the oven
Suitable for freezing

*1 oz. yeast*
*1 c. lukewarm water*
*2–3 tsp. salt*
*1 tbsp. oil*
*4–5 c. all-purpose flour*

1. Dissolve the yeast in lukewarm water. Add salt, oil and most of the flour. Mix thoroughly and knead in the remaining flour until the dough is elastic. Cover and place in a warm spot to rise for about 2 hr.
2. Remove to a floured board, divide into three pieces and form each piece into a ball. Let the balls rest for 4–5 min. before rolling them out into long, thin "sausages." Stop for a few minutes if the dough begins to contract.
3. Cover with a cloth and set aside to rise again on a greased baking sheet for 20–30 min. Brush with lightly salted lukewarm water and make two or three long s-shaped cuts with a razor blade.
4. Place a small ovenproof bowl containing lukewarm water in the bottom of the preheated oven and bake the loaves for 12–15 min. at 475–500°. If you want an extra crisp crust, brush with water during the baking. Cool the loaves on a wire rack.

TIP
### Burned Crust
If the loaves seem to be getting too brown on top, put a piece of paper over them so that they do not burn before they have finished baking.

2 oz. yeast
1½ c. milk
2 tbsp. oil
2 tsp. salt
1 tsp. sugar
4–4½ c. all-purpose flour

1. Dissolve the yeast in lukewarm milk. Add oil, sugar, most of the flour and salt. Mix the dough thoroughly until it is smooth, and knead in the rest of the flour. Cover and set aside in a warm place to rise for about 30 min.
2. Remove the dough to a floured board and divide it in two. Roll one part out to a slab about ½ in. thick. Using a glass, punch out rounds about 3 in. in diameter, and let them rise again for about 20 min. on a greased baking sheet, covered with a cloth or plastic wrap.
3. Collect the pieces of dough that are left over, knead them with the other half of the dough and roll out finger-thick "sausages" about 4 in. long. Cover and leave to rise again for about 20 min. on a greased baking sheet. Brush with water or milk and bake for 15 min. at 400°. Cool on a wire rack.

**Walnut Bread**
(makes 2 loaves)
Preparation time: about 20 min.
Rising time: about 1¼ hr.
Baking time: about 30 min.
Oven temperature: 400–425°
Lowest rack in the oven
Suitable for freezing

2 tbsp. butter or margarine
1 c. water
2 oz. yeast
1½ c. buttermilk
3 tsp. salt
1 c. stone-ground whole-wheat flour
3–4 oz. walnuts
4–4½ c. all-purpose flour

1. Dissolve the yeast in the water. Add lukewarm milk, melted butter, and whole-wheat flour. Add salt. Chop the walnuts finely and stir them into the dough together with most of the all-purpose flour. Mix the dough thoroughly and add more flour until the dough is smooth but not too firm. Cover and set aside to rise in a warm place for 45–50 min. Knead the dough a little after about 20 min.

# Economical and Wholesome

**Viennese Rolls, Hamburger Rolls**
(makes about 24 rolls)
Preparation time: about 20 min.
Rising time: about 50 min.
Baking time: about 15 min.
Oven temperature: 400°
Middle rack in the oven
Suitable for freezing

2. Turn the dough out onto a floured board, form it into two balls, then shape these into ovals. Let these rise for 20–25 min., covered, on a greased baking sheet.

3. Brush the loaves with water or milk. Cut a star pattern with a sharp knife and bake them for about 30 min. at 400–425°. Cool on a wire rack.

### Saffron or Caraway Braids
(makes about 20 kringels)
Preparation time: about 20–25 min.
Rising time: about 1 hr.
Baking time: about 15 min.
Oven temperature: 425°
Middle rack in the oven
Suitable for freezing

$\frac{1}{2}$ c. butter or margarine
$1\frac{1}{2}$ c. milk
1 oz. yeast
1 tsp. salt
1 tsp. sugar
2 eggs
4–$4\frac{1}{2}$ c. all-purpose flour
$\frac{1}{4}$ tsp. saffron
$\frac{1}{2}$–1 tbsp. caraway seeds.

1. Melt the butter and add the milk. Dissolve the yeast in the tepid mixture and add sugar and 1 egg. If making saffron braids, add the saffron; for caraway braids add half the caraway seeds.

2. Stir in salt and half the flour. Knead in the rest of the flour by hand until the dough is smooth and not too firm. Cover and set aside in a warm place to rise for 35–40 min.

3. Remove the dough to a floured board and divide it in 20 portions which should be left to rest for about 5 min. Roll out to long, thin "sausages" and shape into rings or figure eights. Cover, and leave to rise on a greased baking sheet for about 20 min. Brush with beaten egg and sprinkle the caraway braids with the remaining caraway seeds. Bake for 15 min. at 425° and cool on a rack.

### Rusks (right)
(makes about 50 rusks)
Preparation time: about 25 min.
Rising time: about 1 hr.
Baking time: about 12–15 min.
Drying time: 1–2 hr.
Oven temperature: 425 and 225°
Middle rack in the oven

2 oz. yeast

1 c. milk
1 tsp. salt
3 tbsp sugar
1 egg
6 tbsp. butter or margarine
4–$4\frac{1}{2}$ c. all-purpose flour

1. Dissolve the yeast in lukewarm milk, add salt, sugar, egg and half the flour. Mix the dough with a wooden spoon until smooth or use a food mixer with a dough hook for 3–4 min. Cover the dough and put in a warm place to rise for 20 min.

2. Rub the butter into the remaining flour, mix it with the dough which has finished rising and knead thoroughly. Let it rise for 15–20 min. more.

3. Remove the dough to a floured board, divide and shape it into small rounds. Let these rise again on a greased baking sheet for 15–20 min., then bake for 12–15 min. at 425°. Turn the thermostat down to 225°.

4. Divide the buns in two with a fork and lay them on the baking sheet, the cut side up. Let them stay in the oven until they are dry right through and a nice golden color.

## Hard Rolls (white and brown)

(makes about 48 rolls)
Preparation time: about 25 min.
Rising time: about 1 hr.
Baking time: about 10 min.
Drying time: 2–3 hr. at 225° with the oven door ajar
Oven temperature: 450°
Middle rack in the oven

### White Rolls

*2 oz. yeast*
*2 c. milk*
*1 tsp. salt*
*½ c. butter or margarine*
*6 tbsp. sugar*
*8–9 c. all-purpose flour*

### Brown Rolls

*2 oz. yeast*
*2 c. milk*
*1 tsp. salt*
*¾ c. butter or margarine*
*½ c. sugar*
*3–3½ c. stone-ground whole-wheat flour*
*4–4½ c. all-purpose flour*

### Whole-wheat Rolls

*4 oz. yeast*
*2 c. milk*
*1 tsp. salt*
*¾ c. butter or margarine*
*2 tbsp. sugar or maple syrup*
*9–10 c. stone-ground whole-wheat flour*

1. Dissolve yeast in ¼ c. of the lukewarm milk.
2. Rub butter into flour and add salt and sugar or syrup. Add the yeast mixture and the rest of the lukewarm milk and work the dough until it is smooth and firm. Cover and set aside in a warm place for about 30 min. to rise.
3. Remove the dough to a floured board and knead it thoroughly. Divide into about 48 portions (first into 6, then each of these into 8). Shape into round or oval buns. Cover with a cloth and put aside to rise on a greased baking sheet for about 30 min.
4. Bake for about 10 min. at 450° and cool on a wire rack. Turn the thermostat down to about 225°.
5. Split the buns with a fork and place them, cut side up, on the baking sheet. Dry them for 2–3 hr. at the lower temperature with the oven

door a little ajar. Several trays of rolls can be dried at the same time.

### Whole-wheat Buns

(makes 16–18 buns)
Preparation time: about 15–20 min.
Rising time: about 1 hr.
Baking time: about 20 min.
Oven temperature: 400°
Middle rack in the oven
Suitable for freezing

*¾ c. lukewarm water*
*1 tbsp. butter*
*2 oz. yeast*
*¾ c. buttermilk or natural plain yogurt*
*1½–2 tsp. salt*
*1 c. stone-ground whole-wheat flour*
*3–4 c. all-purpose flour*

1. Dissolve the yeast in lukewarm water with the melted butter. Add lukewarm buttermilk or yogurt, salt, whole-wheat flour and most of the all-purpose flour. Mix the dough thoroughly and add more flour until the dough is smooth. Cover and set aside in a warm place to rise for about 40 min.
2. Remove the dough to a floured board and form it into a long roll. Divide it, shape into buns, and place these on a baking sheet to rise again for about 20 min.
3. Brush the buns with water or milk and sprinkle a little coarsely ground whole-wheat flour on top. Bake as directed, then cool on a wire rack.

### Nut Buns

(makes 24 buns)
Preparation time: about 15–20 min.
Rising time: about 50 min.
Baking time: about 18–20 min.
Oven temperature: 400–425°
Middle rack in the oven
Suitable for freezing

*2 oz. yeast*
*2 c. lukewarm water*
*2 tsp. salt*
*1 tsp. sugar*
*1 tbsp. oil*
*3 oz. nuts*
*2 c. stone-ground whole-wheat flour*
*4–5 c. all-purpose flour*

1. Dissolve the yeast in lukewarm water and add salt, sugar, oil, chopped nuts, whole-wheat flour

and most of the all-purpose flour. Mix thoroughly, adding more flour until the dough is smooth. Cover and put in a warm place to rise for 30–35 min.
2. Remove the dough to a floured board and form buns. Place these on a greased baking sheet to rise again, covered, for about 20 min. Brush with water, milk or melted butter, and sprinkle a little whole-wheat flour or chopped nuts on top. Bake for 18–20 min. at 400–425° and cool on a wire rack.

### Flat Breads

(makes about 32 pieces)
Preparation time: about 15 min.
Rising time: about 45 min.
Baking time: 12–15 min.
Oven temperature: 400–425°
Middle rack in the oven
Store in airtight containers

*2 oz. yeast*
*1 c. milk*
*½ c. butter or margarine*
*3–4 c. all-purpose flour*
*¾ c. wholemeal flour*

1. Heat the milk until it is lukewarm. Melt the butter and cool. Dissolve the yeast in ¼ c. of the milk and add the rest of the milk and half the butter. Add most of the flour and stir until the dough is firm. Knead well, cover, and put in a warm place to rise for about 30 min.
2. Work the rest of the butter into the dough and add more flour, if needed. Divide the dough into portions and form evenly shaped buns. Leave them to rise for about 15 min.
3. Roll out the buns into very thin, round "pancakes," preferably with a diamond-patterned or fluted rolling-pin. Punch a little hole in the middle of each. Prick the surface with a fork and bake on a greased baking sheet at 400–425° until a nice golden color. Cool on a wire rack.

### Oven Squares

(makes 24 pieces)
Preparation time: about 15 min.
Rising time: about 30 min.
Baking time: about 15 min.
Oven temperature: 425°
Middle rack in the oven
Suitable for freezing

*Freshly baked Caraway Braids are delicious with coffee or tea.*

of chilled butter over about $\frac{2}{3}$ of the rolled out dough. Fold and roll out as shown on page 49. Repeat the rolling out and folding 3–4 times.

3. When rolling out for the last time, the slab of dough should be oblong-shaped and folded into three, lengthwise. Cut 2–2½ in. wide pieces and place on a greased baking sheet to rise for 30 min. Brush with egg, sprinkle with poppy seeds and bake for 12–15 min. at 425°. Cool on a wire rack.

### Batch Buns

(makes 8 buns)
Preparation time: about 20 min.
Rising time: about 1 hr.
Baking time: about 15–20 min.
Second baking time: 10–12 min.
Oven temperature: 425 and 475°
Middle rack in the oven
Suitable for freezing

2 oz. yeast
1 c. lukewarm water
2 tsp. salt
1 tsp. sugar
1 egg
4–4½ c. all-purpose flour

1. Dissolve the yeast in the lukewarm water. Add sugar, egg, salt and most of the flour. Work the dough until it is smooth and knead in the rest of the flour by hand. Cover and let stand in a warm place to rise for about 40 min.
2. Remove the dough to a floured board and divide it into 8 portions. Make buns and place them closely together in a small, greased 8 × 10 in. pan. Place this pan over a saucepan of boiling water, cover with a cloth or plastic wrap, then move the saucepan from the heat. Leave dough to rise again for 20 min.
3. Brush the buns with water or milk and bake for 15–20 min. at 425°. Split the buns with a fork when they have cooled a little. Place them, cut side up, on a baking sheet and put them back into the oven for about 10–12 min. at 475° until they are golden. Cool on a wire rack.

1 oz. yeast
½ c. milk
1 tsp. salt
3 tbsp. brown sugar
1 tbsp. ground caraway seeds
4–6 c. finely ground whole rye flour
whole caraway seeds for decorating

1. Dissolve the yeast in ¼ c. lukewarm milk. Add sugar, crushed caraway seeds, the remaining milk, and salt. Add the flour and work the dough until smooth.
2. Thoroughly grease a rectangular baking tin and spread the dough evenly over the bottom. Mark into squares with a knife dipped in melted butter, cover and leave in a warm place for about 30 min. until the dough has almost doubled in bulk.
3. Brush top with water and sprinkle over caraway seeds. Bake for 15 min. at 425°.
4. Cool on a wire rack, but break the squares apart before they have cooled

completely.

### Tea Pastries

(makes 14–16 pastries)
Preparation time: about 20–25 min.
Rising time: about 30 min.
Baking time: about 12–15 min.
Oven temperature: 425°
Middle rack in the oven
Suitable for freezing

1 oz. yeast
½ c. milk
2 eggs
1 tsp. salt
1 tsp. sugar
2½–3½ c. all-purpose flour
½ c. butter or margarine
poppy seeds

1. Dissolve the yeast in milk, add 1 egg and sugar. Add salt and enough flour so the dough is soft and smooth.
2. Roll out the dough immediately on a floured board, place thin slices

41

# Sweet Yeast Breads

When you add sugar, butter and perhaps dried fruit to an ordinary dough, the result is fragrant, delicious sweet bread. It is especially good when served freshly baked and still warm. If there is any left over, it can be frozen.

The sugar has a stimulating effect on the yeast cells and causes the dough to rise more quickly. Be careful, therefore, not to let the dough rise for too long, as it could collapse during baking. The butter should, preferably, be rubbed into the flour and not melted. But there are exceptions. Chilled butter can be rolled into dough which has already risen, and the consistency will then be layered, rather like puff pastry. Sweet breads made with yeast dough are often brushed with egg, cream, coffee, milk, melted butter, sugar syrup, or the like. This gives an attractive, shiny surface, and keeps various kinds of decoration in place. The brushing makes the edges of rolled out dough stick together, so that the filling doesn't seep out during the rising and baking process.

These breads baked with yeast are very suitable for freezing, but do not put on any icing or decoration until they have been thawed out. Large loaves should be thawed out at room temperature while still in their wrappings, and be heated a little in the oven at about 350° just before they are to be served; then they will be just as if they were freshly baked. Small loaves can be taken directly from the freezer and thawed in the oven at 375–400°.

On the following pages are recipes for sweet breads and buns. Some of the recipes use the same basic dough, but with different fillings, icing and decoration. It is very labor-saving to make one dough and be able to serve two or three different kinds of breads and buns from it. And everyone, old and young, is fond of this kind of baking.

**Nut Bread** (below)
1 2-lb. loaf tin
Preparation time: about 20 min.
Rising time: about 1 hr.
Baking time: about 35–45 min.
Oven temperature: 400–425°
Lowest rack in the oven
Suitable for freezing

**For the dough:**
*5–6 c. all-purpose flour*
*1 oz. yeast*
*1 c. milk*
*6 tbsp. butter or margarine*

*6 tbsp. sugar*
*2 eggs*
*½ tsp. salt*
*½ lemon*
*1 egg for brushing top*
**For the Filling:**
*7 oz. hazelnuts*
*7 tbsp. sugar*
*1 tsp. vanilla extract*
*2 egg whites*
*egg for brushing*

1. Dissolve yeast in ¼ c. lukewarm milk. Add a little flour to make a very soft sponge. Sprinkle with a little more flour and leave to rise in a warm place for 15 min.

2. Melt butter, remove the saucepan from the heat to let the butter cool a little. Stir in the sugar, beaten eggs, salt, lemon juice and grated lemon peel.

3. Pour this mixture over flour and yeast in the bowl, stir the dough until it is smooth and even, and let it rise for 20–25 min. more.

4. Toast the hazelnuts lightly in a dry frying pan. Grind them or chop them finely. Mix the nuts with the sugar, the two egg whites and the vanilla.

5. Roll out the dough to a fairly thick oblong, spread the filling lengthwise over the dough and brush the edges with beaten egg. Roll the dough together lengthwise and place in the greased tin. Let the bread rise again for 20–25 min. in a warm place, well covered. Brush it with beaten egg and make cuts in the surface to give a diamond pattern. Bake for 35–45 min. at 425° and cool on a wire rack.

## Sugar Braids, Raisin Buns and Small Braids

(makes 16 buns and 12 braids or small braids)
Preparation time: about 15–20 min.
Rising time: about 45 min.
Baking time: 12–15 min.
Oven temperature: 425–475°
Middle rack in the oven
Suitable for freezing

**For the dough:**
*2 oz. yeast*
*½ c. butter*
*¾ c. milk*
*2 tbsp. sugar*
*½ tsp. salt*
*1 egg*
*2 tbsp. buttermilk*
*4–4½ c. all-purpose flour*
**For the decoration:**
*4 tbsp. rock sugar, poppy seeds*
*6 tbsp. raisins*

1. Dissolve crumbled yeast in lukewarm milk, not above 95°. Mix in melted butter. Add sugar, salt, egg and buttermilk, or some other sour milk product, and about half the flour. Work the dough with a wooden spoon until it is smooth. Knead in the rest of the flour by hand. Let the dough stand in a warm place, covered with a cloth or plastic wrap, for

25–30 min. to rise.

2. Knead the dough and divide it into two. Knead raisins into one part and shape buns; put on a baking sheet to rise for 15–20 min.

3. Roll out the remaining dough into strips, and shape into braids (rings or figure eights) or braid three strips together to form small loaves. Put these to rise on a baking sheet and brush with beaten egg. Sprinkle sugar on top of the braids, and poppy seeds on top of the small braided loaves.

Bake for 12–15 min. at 425–475° and cool on a wire rack. All these can be eaten as they are, or with butter and jam.

### Buns

In the illustrations to the right, we have rolled out half the Sugar Braid dough into 16 buns without raisins. They may be baked in the usual way, but can be improved with a little decoration.

*1. Roll out round buns and place them on a greased baking sheet or on waxed paper.*

*2. Clip a cross in each bun, at the same time as you "drag" the scissors a little upward. Let the buns rise and bake, as described in the recipe.*

*3. When the buns are cool, they can be brushed with melted butter and dipped into sugar, sprinkled with powdered sugar, or spread with a thick icing of powdered sugar and milk.*

# Cakes made with Yeast

### Party Raisin Bread
Preparation time: about 25 min.
Rising time: about 40–45 min.
Baking time: about 25 min.
Oven temperature: 425°
Middle rack in the oven
Suitable for freezing

$\frac{1}{2}$ c. butter or margarine
$\frac{1}{2}$ c. milk
1 oz. yeast
2 tbsp. sugar
$\frac{1}{4}$ tsp. salt
$\frac{1}{2}$ tsp. cardamom
$2\frac{1}{2}$–3 c. all-purpose flour
1 egg, beaten
5 tbsp. raisins
$2\frac{1}{2}$ oz. candied orange or lemon peel

1. Melt 1 tbsp. butter, add the milk and dissolve the yeast in the luke-warm mixture. Add sugar, salt, cardamom, $\frac{1}{2}$ the beaten egg and slightly more than half of the flour. Knead the dough until smooth, set it aside to rise in a warm place, well-covered, until about doubled in bulk.
2. Knead in a little more flour, but the dough must not be too firm. Roll it out, cover with remaining butter and fold, as shown on page 49. Roll out and fold altogether 3 times.
3. Roll out again, sprinkle the candied peel and raisins mixed together

over the dough, then roll the dough together and put in into a small round cake pan.
4. Let the bread rise again for about 20 min., brush with remaining egg and bake for 25 min. at 425°.

### Fig Wreath
Preparation time: about 25 min.
Rising time: about 50 min.
Baking time: about 30 min.
Oven temperature: 400°
Middle rack in the oven
Suitable for freezing

**For the dough:**
4–5 c. all-purpose flour
1–2 oz. yeast
1 c. milk
6 tbsp. butter or margarine
2 oz. sugar
juice and rind of $\frac{1}{2}$ lemon
**For the filling and decoration:**
4–6 tbsp. butter or margarine
4 tbsp. sugar
2 oz. almonds
4 tbsp. raisins
$\frac{1}{4}$ lb. dried figs
2 oz. semi-sweet chocolate
$\frac{1}{2}$ c. powdered sugar

1. Dissolve yeast in $\frac{1}{4}$ c. lukewarm milk. Add remaining milk and only enough flour to make a very soft dough. Sprinkle with a little more flour and leave to rise, covered, in a warm place for 15–20 min.
2. Melt the butter and mix it with sugar, lemon juice, and finely grated lemon rind. Pour the mixture into the bowl and work the dough until

smooth. Set aside to rise for about 15–20 min.
3. Chop the almonds coarsely and mix them with the coarsely grated chocolate, chopped figs and raisins.
4. Knead the dough and roll it out to an oblong. Spread the butter for the filling over it and sprinkle sugar, raisins, almonds, chocolate, and figs on top. Roll the dough lengthwise and then cut through it lengthwise with a sharp knife, dipped in flour. Twine the two halves lightly together to form a wreath. Put on a baking sheet to rise again for 15–20 min., and bake for about 30 min. at 400°.
5. Stir powdered sugar and a little warm water to make a smooth icing. Ice the bread while it is still warm and put aside to cool.

### Advent Wreath
Preparation time: about 15–20 min.
Rising time: about 50 min.
Baking time: about 25 min.
Oven temperature: 425°
Middle rack in the oven
Suitable for freezing

**For the dough:**
1 c. milk
2 oz. yeast
6 tbsp. butter or margarine
5 tbsp. sugar
$\frac{1}{2}$ tsp. salt
1 tsp. cardamom
4–$4\frac{1}{2}$ c. all-purpose flour
**For the Filling:**
3–4 tbsp. butter
3 tbsp. sugar

### Coffee Cake with Filling

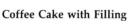

*1. Follow the recipe for Advent Wreath and roll the dough out to fit the baking sheet. Brush the middle with melted butter and spread the filling over.*

*2. Fold the dough into three so that all the filling is covered and fold in the ends. To prevent the edges from gaping, brush a little beaten egg white along them.*

*3. Fold the ends under, and place the cake on a greased baking sheet. Let it rise, and brush and bake it, as explained in the Advent Wreath recipe above.*

½ tsp. cinnamon
1 egg for brushing top
2 oz. almonds for decoration

1. Dissolve the yeast in lukewarm milk. Stir in melted butter, sugar, salt, cardamom and most of the flour. Work the dough until it is smooth, adding more flour, but do not make it hard. Place in a warm place to rise for about 30 min.
2. Remove the dough to a floured board and roll it out to an oblong shape. Spread softened butter for filling on top and sprinkle sugar, cinnamon and 1–2 tbsp. chopped almonds over it. Roll the dough lengthwise and form it into a wreath on a baking sheet covered with waxed paper. Let it rise again for 20 min.
3. Brush the wreath with beaten egg and sprinkle remaining chopped almonds on top. Bake for 25 min. at 425° and cool.

If the wreath is to be used with lighted candles, press candleholders of double foil into the wreath before it is put in the oven. A large, solid candle with tinfoil wrapped around its base, placed in the middle of the wreath when it has been baked and decorated with non-flammable greenery, is an attractive variation.

### Almond Braid
Preparation time: about 20 min.
Rising time: about 1 hr.
Baking time: about 30–40 min.
Oven temperature: 400–425°
Lowest rack in the oven
Suitable for freezing

1 quantity dough as for Nut Bread (see page 44)
5 oz. almonds
4 tbsp. candied orange or lemon peel
3 tbsp. sugar
1 egg for brushing top

*Above: An inviting Fig Wreath, filled with almonds, raisins, figs and chocolate*

1. Make the yeast dough as described for Nut Bread. Blanch the almonds, finely chop half of them, and mix with the candied peel. Knead this mixture into the dough before setting it aside to rise.
2. Knead the dough thoroughly after it has finished rising and divide it into three. Roll each third out into a 12 in. long strip. Braid the strips of dough together and fold the ends in. Let the braid rise again on a greased baking sheet for 20–25 min.
3. Brush the loaf with beaten egg. Chop the remaining almonds coarsely and mix them with the sugar. Spread this on top of and bake for 30–40 min. at 400–425°. Cool on a wire rack.

# Danish Pastries

*Time and care are needed to make Danish pastries, but the results are especially attractive and delicious.*

## Danish Pastries (basic dough)

(makes about 32 small Danish pastries or 2 large)
Preparation time: about 30 min.
Resting time for dough: 20–60 min.
Rising time: about 20 min.
Baking time: (6–8 min. for small Danish pastries, 15–18 min. for long bars, wreaths, etc.)
Baking temperature: 425–475°
Top or middle rack in the oven

*A variety of tempting, fresh Danish pastries*

Suitable for freezing

2 oz. yeast
1 c. cold milk
½ tsp. salt
3 tbsp. sugar
1 egg
4–5 c. all-purpose flour
**To roll out:**
1 c. butter
2 tbsp. all-purpose flour

1. Dissolve the yeast in the cold milk. Add salt, sugar, beaten egg and at least half the flour. Work the dough with a wooden spoon until it is smooth, and knead in the remaining flour, a little at a time. The dough should be smooth but quite soft. Do not handle it any more than is necessary.
2. Roll out the dough as illustrated on page 49 (it is not to rise yet).
3. The dough can now be used in various ways as described in the following recipes. Place the pastries on cold baking sheets, preferably on waxed paper as the filling often seeps out. Cover the pastries well and leave to rise for about 20 min. in a cool place. Bake as directed, remove carefully from the baking sheets and leave to cool on a wire rack.

## Danish Pastries with Fruit Filling

*1 quantity basic dough*
**For the filling:**
½–¾ c. fruit purée or thick jam
3–4 tbsp. heavy cream

1. Roll out the dough to make two 6 × 9 in. oblongs. Put applesauce, apricot jam, preserved prunes, or any other jam or fruit filling in a broad strip down the middle of the dough. Turn in the edges as shown in the drawings on page 46.
2. Set the pastries aside to rise, brush the edges with cream and bake for about 15–18 min. at 425°.

3. The pastries can be brushed with a little warm sugar syrup, made of equal parts of sugar and water, if the surface looks dry after baking. They can also be sprinkled with powdered sugar when cool.

## Butter Cake

Round cake tin, about 8 in. in diameter
½ quantity of basic dough
**For the vanilla cream:**
*2 egg yolks*
*2 tbsp. sugar*
*1 tsp. vanilla sugar*
*1 tbsp. cornstarch*
*¾ c. heavy cream*
*½ c. raisins*
*25 almonds*

1. Roll out the dough to about 6 × 8 in. Stir together the egg yolks, sugar, vanilla sugar, cornstarch and cream in a heavy saucepan and let the mixture gradually come to the boil, stirring continuously. Remove the saucepan from the heat as soon as the cream is thick and smooth. Beat or stir it from time to time while it is cooling.
2. Spread the cold cream filling lengthwise on the dough to within ¾ in. of the edges. Sprinkle raisins on top and roll the dough together. Cut ¾–1¼ in. thick slices and place them with the cut edge up in the greased round cake tin.
3. Set aside to rise, brush with beaten egg and sprinkle almonds on top. Bake at 425° for about 18–20 min. until golden in color.

## Spandau Pastries

(makes 16 pastries)
½ quantity of basic dough
½ quantity vanilla cream (see Butter Bread
    above)
about 5 tbsp. powdered sugar
egg white

1. Roll out the dough to about 12 × 12 in. and cut it into 16 squares. Fold the points in toward the middle, fasten them with a little egg white, and put a little vanilla cream in the middle.
2. Set the pastries aside to rise on a baking sheet. Brush with milk and bake about 6–8 min. at 475°. If you want a shiny surface, brush with a sugar syrup of equal parts powdered sugar dissolved in a little egg white.

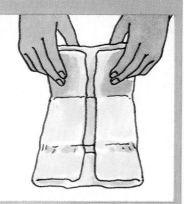

### Rolling out Danish Pastry Dough

*1. Roll out the dough on a lightly floured board to a square about 16 × 16 in. Cut chilled butter into thin slices, put them in the middle of the square and sift a thin layer of flour over.*
*2. Fold the dough in over the butter from the sides, so that you make a parcel.*
*3. With the open side turned away from you, begin the rolling.*

*4. Roll the dough out again carefully to its original size, without using too much force. When the butter begins to be visible, fold the dough again in the same way, make a quarter turn with it and roll out again. Fold and roll out two more times. Let the dough stand in a cold place for 10–20 min. between each rolling out. Form pastries as in recipe. Place them, covered, on a baking sheet and leave in a cool place for about 20 min. to rise.*

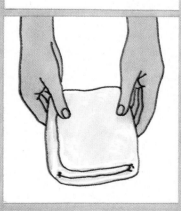

## Stars

(makes 16 stars)
½ quantity of basic dough
**For the filling:**
*½ c. applesauce or thick jam, egg white,
    milk for brushing*
**For the icing:**
*¾ c. powdered sugar, egg white*

1. Roll out the dough to about 12 × 12 in. Cut it into 16 squares and place a spoonful of applesauce or jam on each.
2. Make a diagonal cut in each corner and fold every other point in over the filling. Brush the points with raw egg white so that they stay in place during baking.
3. Place the stars on a baking sheet to rise, brush with milk and bake for about 6–8 min. at 475°. Make an icing of sugar and a little raw egg white and drip a little in the middle of each star when they are cool.

**Lord Mayor's Cake**

*1. Place the filling down the middle of the rolled out rectangle of dough.*

*2. Make diagonal cuts on both sides of the dough, about ¾ in. apart*

*3. Fold the strips in over the filling, alternately from the right and left.*

**Lord Mayor's Cake**
*½ quantity basic dough*
*4 oz. almonds*
*¾ c. powdered sugar*
*1 egg (separated)*
*1 tbsp. heavy cream*

1. Roll out the dough to a 6 × 8 in. rectangle. Blanch the almonds, sliver about a third of them and grind or finely chop the rest. Mix the ground almonds with the sugar and egg white and lay the filling in a strip lengthwise on the dough.
2. Make cuts as shown in the diagrams; or fold the dough over the filling, make cuts along the whole length of the dough and draw the cut portions a little out to the side.
3. Set aside to rise, brush with a mixture of egg yolk and cream, and sprinkle the slivered almonds over the top. Bake at 425° for about 15–18 min., until the bread is crisp and golden in color.

**Cocks' Combs**
(makes about 16 pastries)
*½ quantity basic dough*
*6 tbsp. butter or margarine*
*¾ c. powdered sugar*
*2 oz. almonds*
*1 egg for brushing top*
*granulated sugar*

1. Roll the dough out to a rectangle about 12 × 20 in. Stir softened butter together with the sugar and at least half the blanched and finely chopped almonds.

2. Place the filling in a broad strip in the middle of the rectangle and fold both sides to the center with a slight overlap. Slice into pieces about 1½–2 in. wide and make 4–5 cuts in the top edge of each. Curve the cakes so that the cuts open wider.
3. Place the pastries on a baking sheet and set them aside to rise again. Brush with egg and sprinkle top with chopped almonds and granulated sugar. Bake about 6–8 min. at 475°.

**Cream Buns**
(makes 16 buns)
*½ quantity basic dough*
*½ quantity vanilla cream (see Butter Cake, page 49)*
*1 egg for brushing top*
*¾ c. powdered sugar*

1. Roll the dough out into a square about 12 × 12 in. Cut it into 16 squares and place a little vanilla cream on each.
2. Fold the corners in over the filling, press them lightly together and place the buns, with the seam underneath, on a baking sheet. Set aside to rise.
3. Brush the buns with beaten egg and bake them until golden at 475°.
4. Brush the warm buns with a little sugar syrup made of equal parts of water and sugar. Sprinkle powdered sugar on top.

**Birthday Braid**
Preparation time: about 20 min.
Rising time: about 50 min.

Baking time: about 25–30 min.
Oven temperature: 425°
Middle rack in the oven
Suitable for freezing

**For the dough:**
*3–4 c. all-purpose flour*
*½ tsp. salt*
*1 tsp. cardamom*
*1 c. butter or margarine*
*1 oz. yeast*
*½ c. milk*
*2 eggs*
*2 tbsp. sugar*
**For the filling and decoration:**
*½ c. butter*
*7 tbsp. sugar*
*2 oz. almonds*
*4 tbsp. raisins*
*2 tbsp. candied lemon or lime peel*
*1 egg*
*sugar*

1. Mix flour, salt and cardamom, and rub the butter into the flour with your finger tips. Dissolve the yeast in lukewarm milk and beat the eggs with the sugar. Pour both into the flour, mix the dough with a wooden spoon until it is smooth and elastic and set it aside, covered, in a warm place for about 30 min. to rise.
2. Combine the softened butter for the filling with the sugar, 1 oz. blanched and finely chopped almonds, raisins, and finely chopped candied peel.
3. Remove the dough to a floured board and knead it. Divide it into two and roll each portion into a rec-

tangle. Place the filling in a strip down the middle and fold the sides in over the filling so that it is covered.

4. Form the pastries into a braided ring or figure eight on a greased baking sheet. Press the seams tightly together and set the braid aside to rise for about 20 min. Brush with beaten egg and sprinkle sugar and chopped almonds. Bake about 25–30 min. at 425° and cool a little on the baking sheet before transferring to a wire rack.

## Jam Pastries
(makes 16 pastries)
*½ quantity basic dough*
*½ c. jam*
*¾ c. powdered sugar*
*egg whites and milk for brushing*

1. Roll out the dough to a square about 12 × 12 in. and cut it into 16 squares. Place a little thick jam in the middle of each square, and fold two opposite corners of dough in over the filling. Fasten them with egg white and press them well together.
2. Set the pastries aside on a baking sheet to rise. Brush with milk and bake them for about 6–9 min. at 475° or until they are golden.
3. Decorate the cooled pastries with a glaze of powdered sugar dissolved in a little egg white.

## Saffron Braid
Preparation time: about 20 min.
Rising time: about 45–50 min.
Baking time: about 25 min.
Oven temperature: 400–425°
Lowest rack in the oven
Suitable for freezing

*6 tbsp. butter or margarine*
*1 c. lukewarm milk*
*1 oz. yeast*
*½ tsp. salt*
*3–4 tbsp. sugar*
*1 egg*
*¼ tsp. saffron*
*1 tbsp. grated lemon rind*
*4–4½ c. all-purpose flour*
*1 egg yolk for brushing top*

1. Melt the butter, add a little of the milk. Dissolve the yeast in the lukewarm mixture.
2. Add salt, sugar, egg, saffron, lemon rind, the remaining milk, and the flour a little at a time. Work the dough until it is smooth and elastic and cover and store in a warm place to rise for about 30 min.
3. Remove the dough to a floured board and divide it into three. Form each portion into a ball and let it stand for 5 min. Roll the balls out into 20–

*Saffron Braid, golden and tempting*

24 in. long "sausages" and braid them together. Make a ring or figure eight of the braid and cover and put to rise on a greased baking sheet for 20 min. Brush with the egg yolk beaten with 1 tbsp. water. Bake for about 25 min. at 400–425° and cool on a wire rack.

**Filled Crescent Rolls (basic recipe)**

(makes about 24 crescents)
Preparation time: about 25 min.
Rising time: about 50 min.
Baking time: about 15 min.
Oven temperature: 400–425°
Middle rack in the oven
Suitable for freezing without icing and decoration

*2 oz. yeast*
*¾ c. light cream*
*1 egg*
*1 tsp salt*
*1 tbsp. sugar*
*2 tbsp. sour cream*
*½ c. butter or margarine*
*4–4½ c. all-purpose flour*

1. Dissolve the yeast in lukewarm cream and add egg, sugar and sour cream. Rub the butter into about 4 c. flour, add salt, and pour the yeast mixture over. Knead the dough until elastic, adding a little more flour. Cover and put aside to rise for about 30 min.

2. Remove the dough to a floured board and roll out. Cut out triangles and put filling on each. Roll up from the broadest side, bend the crescents into a curve and place them on a greased baking sheet with the point of the dough facing down. Let them rise again for 20 min. Bake according to directions and place on a wire rack to cool.

**Suggestions for filling:**
**Cinnamon Crescents**
Stir together 4 tbsp. softened butter,

on the crescents, roll up, bake as directed and cool. Make a thick glaze of $\frac{3}{4}$ c. powdered sugar and the rest of the egg white. Spread the icing on the crescents.

### Mocha Crescents

Stir together a filling made of 2 tbsp. softened butter, 3 tbsp. sugar, 1 tsp. cocoa and 1 tbsp. instant coffee. Fill the crescents, roll up, and bake. Decorate the cooled crescents with an icing made of about $\frac{3}{4}$ c. powdered sugar and a little strong coffee.

### Shrovetide Buns

(makes 20–25 buns)
Preparation time: about 30 min.
Rising time: about 1 hr.
Baking time: 12–15 min.
Oven temperature: 425–450°
Middle rack in the oven
Suitable for freezing, without cream

### For the dough:

6 tbsp. butter or margarine
1 c. milk
1 oz. yeast
4 tbsp. sugar
$\frac{1}{2}$ tsp. salt
1 egg yolk
4–4$\frac{1}{2}$ c. all-purpose flour

### For the filling and decoration:

5 oz. almonds
2 egg whites
4 tbsp. milk
7 tbsp. sugar
1 egg yolk for brushing top
2 c. heavy cream
powdered sugar

1. Melt the butter and stir in the warm milk. Dissolve the yeast in about $\frac{1}{2}$ c. of the lukewarm liquid and add sugar, egg yolk, the rest of the lukewarm milk and most of the flour. Add salt. Stir the dough thoroughly and add more flour until the dough is smooth and not too firm. Cover and set aside in a warm place for 30–35 min. to rise.
2. Remove the dough to a floured board and divide and shape it into even-sized buns. Let these rise again under a cloth on a greased baking sheet for 25–30 min.
3. Brush with egg yolk beaten with 1 tbsp. water or milk. Bake for 12–15 min. at 425–450° and cool on a wire rack.
4. Cut the top off the buns, take out barely half of the insides, and mois-

ten with the milk for filling. Beat egg whites until stiff and carefully mix in the blanched and ground almonds and the moistened dough from the buns. Spread this filling in the buns, put whipped cream on top of each and place the "lid" loosely on top. Sift powdered sugar over the tops.

### Berlin Buns (left)

(makes 20–24 buns)
Preparation time: about 20–25 min.
Rising time: about 50–55 min.
Baking time: about 5–6 min. per bun
Suitable for freezing

2 oz. yeast
$\frac{1}{2}$ c. milk
1 tsp. salt
3 tbsp. sugar
2 tbsp. oil
2 tbsp. rum or lemon juice
1 egg + 1 egg yolk
4–4$\frac{1}{2}$ c. all-purpose flour
jam or crushed fruit
oil for deep frying
sugar or powdered sugar

1. Dissolve the yeast in lukewarm milk. Add salt, sugar, oil, rum or lemon juice and the beaten egg and egg yolk. Add the flour a little at a time, stir thoroughly as long as the dough is sticky, then knead in the rest of the flour by hand. Cover and leave in a warm place for 30–35 min. to rise.
2. Remove the dough to a floured board and roll it out into two rectangles about $\frac{1}{2}$ in. thick. With a glass, outline rounds about 2$\frac{1}{2}$ in. in diameter on one rectangle of dough and put 1–2 tsp. jam in the middle of each round. Lay the other rectangle of dough on top and press the glass through both layers of dough. Use a glass with thick edges, so the buns will stick together better during the baking.
3. Cover and let the buns stand in a warm place to rise for about 20 min. Heat oil in a saucepan to 350–360° or until a cube of bread turns pale brown in 1 min. Put in 3–4 buns at a time and fry them until light brown.
4. Remove the buns with a slotted spoon and drain on paper towels. Roll them in sugar or powdered sugar and serve them hot or lukewarm.

4 tbsp. sugar and $\frac{1}{2}$ tbsp. cinnamon. Fill the crescents, roll up, brush with beaten egg. Sprinkle cinnamon and sugar on top. Bake as directed.

### Apple Crescents

Put 1–2 tsp. thick applesauce on the triangles. Roll them up, bake according to directions, and sprinkle over a thin layer of powdered sugar.

### Marzipan Crescents

Stir 4 oz. grated marzipan with about $\frac{1}{2}$ raw egg white. Spread the filling

# Sheet Cakes

*Crumb Cake with Apricots (above); Tosca Cake (below)*

## Basic Dough

1 shallow pan, 12 × 16 in.
Preparation time: about 15 min.
Rising time: about 30 min.
Baking time and oven temperature:
(see recipes)
Middle rack in the oven
Suitable for freezing

4–4½ c. all-purpose flour
½ c. butter or margarine
3 tbsp. sugar
grated rind of ½ lemon
2 oz. yeast
1 c. milk

1. Sift the flour into a bowl and rub in the butter with your finger tips. Sprinkle in sugar and lemon rind.
2. Dissolve the yeast in lukewarm milk. Pour it into the flour mixture and stir the dough until it is smooth and elastic. Put a cloth or plastic wrap over the bowl and let the dough rise in a warm place until it has doubled in bulk.
3. Line the pan with waxed paper. Knead the dough after it has finished rising and place it in the pan.
4. This base can be left to rise for 20 min. on its own, or the filling can be spread over the top right away and the complete cake baked.

## Crumb Cake with Apricots

Preparation time: about 25 min.
Rising time: about 30 min.
Baking time: about 20–25 min.
Oven temperature: 400°
Suitable for freezing

1 quantity Basic Dough
2 10-oz. cans of apricots
2–2½ c. all-purpose flour
¾ c. sugar
2 tsp. vanilla sugar
1 c. butter or margarine

1. Make the dough and place in greased or waxed paper-lined pan. Drain the apricots well.
2. Mix flour, sugar and vanilla sugar. Rub in chilled butter with the tips of your fingers, or melt it and drip it into the flour mixture, stirring all the while, so that the mixture is crumbly.
3. Place the apricots, round sides up, on top of the yeast dough and spread the crumb on top. Let the cake rise again for 15–20 min., or bake it right away. Cool and slice.

### Cream Cake with Peaches
(right)
Preparation time: about 25–30 min.
Rising time: about 40 min.
Baking time: about 35–40 min.
Oven temperature: 400–425°

*1 quantity Basic Dough*
*2 10-oz. cans of halved peaches*
*1¾ c. cottage cheese*
*3 eggs*
*3 tbsp. cornstarch*
*4 tbsp. sugar*
*½ lemon*
*2 oz. almonds*

1. Make the dough and put it in a greased or lined pan. Drain the peaches well through a sieve.
2. Stir in cottage cheese with beaten eggs, cornstarch, sugar, lemon juice and grated lemon rind.
3. Spread the cheese mixture over the dough and place the peaches on top. Sprinkle blanched, chopped almonds over and let the cake rise for 10 min. Bake, and cut into slices when cool.

### Tosca Cake
Preparation time: about 20 min.
Rising time: about 30 min.
Baking time: 20–25 min.
Oven temperature: 425°
Suitable for freezing

*1 quantity Basic Dough*
*¾ c. butter or margarine*
*4½–5 oz. almonds*
*½ c. sugar*
*2 tsp. vanilla sugar*

1. Make the dough and put it in a greased or paper-lined pan. Prick with a fork, so that bubbles will not form during the baking.
2. Cut chilled butter into slices and lay these on top of the dough. Blanch the almonds, sliver them and sprinkle them over the butter. Sprinkle sugar and vanilla sugar on top. Bake, and cut into slices when cool.

### Cream Slice with Crisp Meringue (right)
Preparation time: about 25 min.
Rising time: about 40 min.
Baking time: about 30–40 min.
Oven temperature: 400–425°
Suitable for freezing

*1 quantity Basic Dough*

*9 tbsp. butter or margarine*
*3 eggs, separated*
*¾ c. sugar*
*1 lemon*
*7 oz. almonds*

1. Make the yeast dough and put it into a greased or lined pan. Let it rise again for about 10 min.
2. Mix softened butter very gradually with egg yolks, blanched and finely chopped almonds, ½ c. sugar and finely grated lemon rind. Spread the mixture over the dough. Beat the egg whites until stiff, fold in the remaining sugar and spread this meringue over the creamy filling. The meringue mixture and the butter cream can also be mixed and spread over the cake together. Bake according to directions and cut the cake into slices when cold.

3. Stir in the yeast mixture and add flour to the dough until it is soft and elastic. Beat the egg whites until they are very stiff and fold them carefully into the dough.

4. Put the dough into the well-greased and floured mold, cover with a damp cloth or plastic wrap and let it rise for about 1 hr. Bake as directed. Test the cake with a thin wooden skewer. The cake is ready when the skewer comes out dry. Turn onto a wire rack to cool.

### Cinnamon Cake with Apples
1 deep, ring mold
Preparation time: about 20 min.
Rising time: about $1\frac{1}{2}$ hr.
Baking time: $1-1\frac{1}{4}$ hr.
Oven temperature: 350–375°
Lowest rack in the oven
Suitable for freezing

2 oz. yeast
$\frac{3}{4}$ c. milk
$4-4\frac{1}{2}$ c. all-purpose flour
$\frac{1}{2}$ c. butter or margarine
$\frac{1}{2}$ c. brown sugar
1 tsp. cinnamon
$\frac{1}{2}$ tsp. ginger
$\frac{1}{2}$ tsp. powdered cloves
1 egg
2 medium apples

1. Dissolve the yeast in $\frac{1}{2}$ c. luke-warm milk. Rub the butter into the flour and add sugar and spices.
2. Pour the yeast mixture and the beaten egg into the flour. Knead the dough and add more milk until it is soft and elastic. Add the peeled, grated apples and leave dough aside to rise until doubled in bulk.
3. Knead the dough lightly and put it into a well-greased, floured tin. Let rise again for about 30 min., then bake as directed. Cool on a wire rack.

### Sister Cake
1 deep, ring mold
Preparation time: about 15 min.
Rising time: about 1 hr.
Baking time: about 40–45 min.
Oven temperature: 400°
Lowest rack in the oven
Suitable for freezing

10 tbsp. butter
4 tbsp. sugar
1 egg
1 oz. yeast
$\frac{1}{2}$ c. milk
$3-3\frac{1}{2}$ c. all-purpose flour

# Ring Mold Cakes

### Gugelhupf
1 deep ring mold
Preparation time: about 25 min.
Rising time: about 1 hr.
Baking time: about 40–45 min.
Oven temperature: 400–425°
Lowest rack in the oven
Suitable for freezing

$2\frac{1}{2}$ oz. raisins
3 tbsp. rum
2 oz. yeast
$\frac{1}{2}$ c. milk
$\frac{3}{4}$ c. butter or margarine
5 egg yolks
9 tbsp. sugar
3 egg whites
$\frac{1}{2}$ lemon
2 tbsp. heavy cream
3–4 c. all-purpose flour

1. Soak the raisins in the rum. Dissolve the yeast in lukewarm milk.
2. Beat butter and sugar until light and fluffy and stir in the egg yolks one at a time. Add raisins, lemon juice and rind, cream and about 1 c. flour.

1 tsp. cardamom
5 tbsp. raisins
2 tbsp. candied lemon or orange peel
powdered sugar

1. Stir the butter and sugar until light and fluffy. Stir in the egg together with 1–2 tbsp. flour. Dissolve the yeast in lukewarm milk.
2. Stir the yeast liquid into the butter mixture and add remaining flour, cardamom, raisins, and chopped candied peel. Work the dough until it is smooth and elastic and put it into the greased and floured tin.
3. Cover the tin with a damp cloth or plastic wrap and let the dough rise for 1 hr. in a warm place. Bake as directed. Turn the cake out onto a wire rack and sift sugar on top.

## Chocolate Ring
1 deep, ring mold
Preparation time: about 25 min.

Rising time: about 35–40 min.
Baking time: about 40–50 min.
Oven temperature: 350°
Lowest rack in the oven
Suitable for freezing before icing

3–3½ c. all-purpose flour
1 oz. yeast
½ c. milk
½ c. sugar
3 eggs
¾ c. butter or margarine
½ lemon
5 oz. currants
**For the icing:**
2 tbsp. butter
4 oz. semi-sweet chocolate
blanched almonds or other nuts for decoration

1. Dissolve yeast in lukewarm milk. Stir in about 1 c. flour. Cover and set aside to rise for about 15 min.
2. Work in the sugar, the beaten eggs, softened butter, grated lemon rind, and the rest of the flour, as needed, so that the dough becomes soft and elastic. Set aside to rise for 20–25 min.
3. Meanwhile, rinse the currants in warm water and dry them well. Work them quickly into the dough and pour it into the well-greased and floured ring mold. Bake as directed and turn out onto a wire rack to cool.
4. Break the chocolate into pieces and melt over hot water, then add the butter and stir until shiny. Spread the icing carefully over the cake and let it harden in a cool place. Decorate with almonds or other nuts before the icing has hardened.

*Chocolate Ring is delightful – both in taste and appearance*

# From Far-off Places

*Many countries have traditions and specialties in yeast baking. Here is a selection.*

## Poppy Cake (opposite)
1 2-lb. loaf tin
Preparation time: about 30 min.
Rising time: about 1 hr.
Baking time: about 30–40 min.
Oven temperature: 400°
Lowest rack in the oven
Suitable for freezing

### For the dough:
1 oz. yeast
1 c. milk
1 egg
1 tsp. salt
6 tbsp. butter or margarine
4–4½ c. all-purpose flour

### For the filling:
½ c. poppy seeds
¾ c. light cream
1 oz. almonds
4 tbsp. sugar
1 tsp. vanilla sugar
2 tbsp. butter
1 egg for brushing top

1. Dissolve the yeast in lukewarm milk. Stir in the egg, sugar, salt, melted butter and most of the flour. Work the dough with a wooden spoon until it is smooth. Knead in more flour by hand. The dough should be fairly soft. Cover and set aside in a warm place to rise until just about doubled in bulk.
2. Grind the poppy seeds in a mortar. Grind the almonds, mix them with the poppy seeds in a saucepan, place over low heat and add cream, a little at a time, until the mixture is about as thick as oatmeal. Stir in sugar, vanilla sugar and butter.
3. Knead the dough lightly, roll it out and spread the filling on top. Roll the dough lengthwise and put into the greased tin. Let the cake rise again for 20–25 min. Brush with beaten egg, make a cut lengthwise with a sharp knife, and bake as directed. Cool on a wire rack.

### VARIATION
Instead of poppy seeds, the cake can be filled with a nut cream, as in the left of the picture. The cream is made with ¼ lb. nuts, finely chopped or ground. Add beaten egg white a little at a time until the mixture is smooth. Sweeten with powdered sugar and flavor with a little rum or liqueur. Coffee liqueur gives very good flavor to this cake.

**Savarin** (opposite right)
1 deep, ring mold
Preparation time: about 25 min.
Rising time: about ¾ hr.
Baking time: about 25–30 min.
Oven temperature: 400–425°
Middle rack in the oven
Suitable for freezing without filling

**For the dough:**
¾ c. butter or margarine
1 oz. yeast
½ c. light cream
4 eggs
2 tbsp. sugar
½ tsp. salt
2–2½ c. all-purpose flour
**For the sugar syrup:**
1 c. water
¾ c. sugar
2–3 tbsp. orange liqueur

1. Melt the butter and cool it a little. Add the cream and dissolve crumbled yeast in the mixture. Add the eggs, one at a time, stirring well between each addition. Then stir in sugar, salt and flour. Work the dough until smooth. Cover with a damp cloth or plastic wrap and put it aside to rise in a warm place for 40–45 min.
2. Boil sugar and water together for 15–20 min. to make the syrup. Do not stir. It should be thick, but the sugar must not be allowed to crystallize. Remove the saucepan from the heat and add the liqueur.
3. Lightly knead the dough which has now finished rising, and put it into the well-greased mold. Bake as directed, turn the cake out carefully onto a wire rack and wash the tin.
4. Put the cake back into the tin and prick holes all over it with, for example, a knitting needle. Pour the sugar syrup over little by little, so that the cake absorbs it gradually. Let the cake stand in a cool place for at least 2–3 hr.
5. Turn the cake out onto a serving dish and fill it with cut-up fresh fruit which has been soaking in a marinade of sweet white wine or sugar syrup with a little liqueur added.

**Baba au Rhum**
1 ring mold
Preparation time: about 20 min.
Rising time: about 1 hr.
Baking time: about 30 min.
Oven temperature: 425 and 350°
Middle rack in the oven

Suitable for freezing but quality will diminish

**For the dough:**
1 oz. yeast
½ c. milk
4 eggs
2 tbsp. sugar
½ tsp. salt
vanilla extract
3–3½ c. all-purpose flour
1 tbsp. white rum
½ c. butter or margarine
**For the sugar syrup:**
1 c. water
1 c. sugar
2–3 tbsp. white rum

1. Dissolve the yeast in lukewarm milk. Beat the eggs with the sugar and stir in the yeast mixture together with the salt, vanilla extract to taste, flour and rum. Stir this soft dough until elastic. Sliver the butter on top and put the dough, covered, in a warm place to rise.
2. Knead the dough with the butter which should now be half melted. Put it into the well-greased and floured ring mold. Let it rise again for about 20 min. Bake for 10 min. at 425° and then at 350° until the cake is baked through.
3. Make a thick sugar syrup of water and sugar, turn off the heat and add the rum. Turn the cake out onto a wire rack and wash the mold.
4. Put the cake back into the mold immediately after cooling and, using a knitting needle, prick it all over with small holes. Drip the rum syrup over the cake several times.
5. Cool the cake and let it stand for 2–3 hr. to absorb the syrup thoroughly. Serve it with whipped or sour cream.

# Baking on a Large Scale

*There is every reason to start baking on a grand scale when you have flour at hand and the oven is warm – and you have the time and the energy. Allow 3 hr., roll up your sleeves and follow the timetable below.*

The following is a good selection for this large-scale bake:
*2 coarse Farmer's Bread loaves (see page 17)*
*2 Round Wheat Breads (see page 37)*
*1 large yeast wreath (the recipe for the Advent Wreath is on pages 46–47) and/or 24 buns with different fillings.*
There will be time enough for both the Advent Wreath and the buns, if you want to make them. Make a double quantity of dough, and make the bread doughs about ½ hr. later than the recipe states.

## Before You Start
Read through the recipes carefully and check that you have everything you need at hand.

Let everything stand in the kitchen for a while – ingredients, bowls etc., so that they are at room temperature. It is very important that nothing that you are going to use is cold. Be sure to have ready either waxed paper or melted butter and a brush for greasing warm baking sheets.

## Suggestions for Fillings:
1. ¼ lb. ground almonds mixed with 3 tbsp. powdered sugar and ½–1 egg white.
2. 3 tbsp. softened butter or margarine, mixed with 3 tbsp. powdered sugar, 1 tbsp. cinnamon and 5 tbsp. raisins.
3. ½ c. thick applesauce or thick jam.
4. 3 tbsp. softened butter or margarine, mixed with 3 tbsp. powdered sugar, 1 tbsp. grated lemon rind and 1–2 tsp. vanilla sugar.
5. 2 tbsp. butter or margarine, 5 tbsp. raisins and 3 tbsp. chopped candied citrus peel.

## First Hour
First make the dough for the Advent Wreath and/or the buns, and put it aside to rise for about 30 min.

Make a double quantity of basic dough for the Round Wheat Bread and set it to rise for about 45 min. Note the exact time for each dough. It is so easy to forget when the dough has been put aside to rise.

Make the filling for the Advent

**Raisins and Candied Peel Buns**

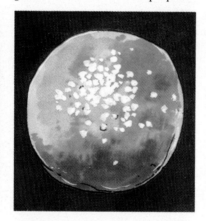

**Filled Buns**

**Clipped Buns**

*Knead Filling No. 5 into a quantity of dough, form buns, let them rise again and brush with egg yolk.*
*All buns are cooked at 450–475°.*

*Form the buns, make a hollow and put in 1 tsp. of Filling No. 1. Pull the dough over the filling, allow to rise again, brush with egg and sprinkle coarse sugar on top.*

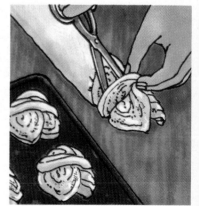

*Roll out the dough to a rectangle and spread on Filling No. 4. Roll lengthwise and cut slices and clip three incisions in each. Fold the incisions outward a little, let dough rise again and brush with egg.*

Wreath. Choose one or several kinds of filling for the buns and get everything ready. Make dough for Farmer's Bread, and let it rise. Remove the dough for the Advent Wreath to a floured board and roll it out into a rectangle. Fill it and form a wreath, and put this aside to rise again on a baking sheet. Or divide the dough into 24 pieces if you want to make filled buns.

### Second Hour

Heat the oven and set the thermostat at 425°. Fill and shape the buns (see detailed drawings at the foot of the page). Set them aside to rise for about 12–15 min.

Remove the Wheat Bread dough to a floured board, divide it in two and form round or oblong loaves, as you wish. Set them on a greased baking sheet to rise again for 20–25 min.

Brush and sprinkle the Advent Wreath or the buns with coarse sugar and put on baking sheets in the oven on the middle rack. The buns may be baked at about 475° for 12–15 min.

Remove the dough for the Farmer's Bread to a floured board, divide it in two and form round loaves and set aside to rise again on a greased baking sheet for about 30 min.

The Advent Wreath should now have finished baking and can be taken from the oven.

### Third Hour

Turn the oven down to 400–425°. Brush the Wheat Bread loaves and put them in the oven on the lowest rack. While the wheat loaves are baking in the oven, you will have plenty of time to begin to tidy up and wash everything before the Farmer's Bread loaves need to be brushed on top and baked.

Remove the Wheat Bread loaves when they have finished baking and put them on a rack to cool.

Brush over the tops of the Farmer's Bread loaves and bake them. Wrap the baked products which are to be frozen before they have cooled completely.

| | Time-table for Large-scale Baking | | | | | |
|---|---|---|---|---|---|---|
| | **Advent Wreath** | | **Wheat Bread** | | **Farmer's Bread** | |
| **1st hr** | 00 | | 00 | | 00 | |
| | 10 | } Make dough | 10 | | 10 | |
| | 20 | } 1st rising | 20 | } Make dough | 20 | |
| | 30 | } Make filling | 30 | | 30 | |
| | 40 | | 40 | | 40 | } Make dough |
| | 50 | } Form wreath | 50 | } 1st rising | 50 | |
| | 60 | | 60 | | 60 | |
| | | } 2nd rising | | | | } 1st rising |
| **2nd hr** | 10 | | 10 | } Form loaves | 10 | |
| | 20 | } Brushing and baking | 20 | | 20 | |
| | 30 | | 30 | } 2nd rising | 30 | |
| | 40 | | 40 | | 40 | } Form loaves |
| | 50 | | 50 | } Brushing and baking | 50 | } 2nd rising |
| | 60 | | 60 | | 60 | |
| **3rd hr** | 10 | | 10 | | 10 | |
| | 20 | | 20 | | 20 | |
| | 30 | | 30 | | 30 | } Brushing and baking |
| | 40 | | 40 | | 40 | |
| | 50 | | 50 | | 50 | |
| | 60 | | 60 | | 60 | |

**Raisin Snails**

**Twisted Buns**

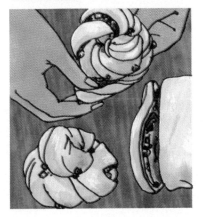

*Roll out the dough to a rectangle and spread on Filling No. 2. Roll up, cut slices and turn in the ends. Leave to rise again, brush with sugared water and sprinkle sugar on top.*

*Roll out the dough to a rectangle and spread on Filling No. 2 or No. 3. Roll up, twist the roll a quarter turn, cut slices and twist them. Allow to rise, brush with egg and sprinkle on sugar.*

# Storing Bread and Other Baked Products

*Baked goods taste best the same day they are made, but there are not many people who have time to bake every day. If you want to preserve the flavor and consistency as nearly as possible, it is important to store it correctly.*

## Bread Box or Refrigerator?

Breads containing a lot of fine flour, such as white bread, rolls, buns etc., can be kept for 1–3 days in a plastic bag in the bread box.

When this bread begins to seem old and dry, it is due partly to drying out and partly to changes in the content of the starch. This occurs most rapidly at 36–37° F and therefore this kind of baked product should never be kept in the refrigerator.

Coarser types of bread such as rye bread and the like can, on the other hand, keep for over a week, tightly wrapped in plastic in the refrigerator. The bread becomes a little firmer in consistency and easier to cut than when it was newly baked. Breads baked of sourdough or the coarsest types of flour keep fresh even longer than ordinary rye breads. Dinner rolls, hard rolls, crescents, etc. can be freshened up by brushing them with cold water and putting them into the oven for a few minutes at 400–425°. Formation of mold on baked products can be a problem, especially in summer. Mold fungus thrives in warmth and dampness, and it is therefore very important that all baked products are completely cooled before they are put into the bread box. Always put your baking on a wire rack to cool. This allows the dampness and heat to escape as quickly as possible. Never eat moldy bread, and do not let pets eat it either. Mold is not directly poisonous, but it can cause stomach upset.

## The Freezer

Freezing is absolutely the best way to store bread and other baked products. At 0 to −12°F almost all development in baked products stops, and the baked goods seem almost freshly baked when thawed. Light types of bread are packed in deep-freeze wrappings while they are lukewarm, then are cooled completely and put into the freezer. The reason for wrapping the bread while it is lukewarm is so the crust doesn't fall off easily from the rest of the bread when it is thawed.

It is best to freeze breads which have been completely baked, but it is possible to freeze bread which has been just shaped and risen. However, the bread must then be made with a double quantity of yeast.

If you do not use very much bread, it may pay to divide large loaves or cut slices, and freeze one or two days' supply.

## Wrapping

Special heavy aluminum foil containers are available in different sizes and shapes for baking and freezing. Bread and cakes can be baked in these molds, which do not need to be greased. After the baked products have cooled, the molds are put into plastic bags especially suited for freezing, and tightly closed. With careful use, the molds can be used several times. Plastic and foil especially intended for freezing make good wrappings for yeast baking. You can write with a pen on special freezing tape. It is very important to write the freezing date on all baked products.

Do not use ordinary plastic bags for freezing; they are too thin and the baked products can dry out and be frost damaged.

Large cakes, braids, Danish pastries and the like should be protected with a piece of cardboard underneath. This is to avoid breakage or damage when you move baked goods in the freezer.

## Freezing Process

It is important to freeze baked goods as quickly as possible in order to retain their freshness and taste. Set the thermostat on the freezer or freezing compartment to its coldest well ahead of time. Put the baked goods in the coldest section or as near the freezing elements as possible. The temperature should preferably be at least −12° F.

## How Long to Keep in Freezer

Bread with very little fat content keeps well for about 6 months when the temperature in the freezer or freezing compartment is at least 0°. Cakes, raw dough and breads with high fat contents should not be kept for more than 3–4 months at the above-mentioned temperature.

## Thawing-out

Whole loaves and cakes are best thawed out in their wrappings at room temperature. An exception to this rule is French Bread which is best thawed in the oven at 425–475° for 8–10 min. Bread which has been thawed can be heated for 5–10 min. in the oven at 400° to freshen up the crust, but note that bread that has been frozen dries out more quickly than freshly baked bread.

Buns, small dinner rolls, and the like should be thawed in their wrappings at room temperature or in the oven. Bread which has been frozen in slices should be thawed in its wrapping in the refrigerator.

Thawing out frozen baked goods:
*At room temperature:*

| | |
|---|---|
| Whole loaves and large cakes: | 3–5 hr. |
| Sliced bread: | 15–20 min. |
| Buns, hard rolls and similar: | 30–60 min. |

*In the oven (approximate time):*
Whole loaves: 45 min. at 350°
Sweet Yeast Breads: 25 min. at 400°
Small loaves: 10 min. at 400°

*Rapid thawing:*
In an emergency you can put frozen slices of bread in the toaster for a couple of minutes.

# Index